How to Direct a Musical

BROADWAY—
YOUR WAY!

Marius, Panisse, and Cesar from *Fanny,* directed by the author.

How to Direct a Musical

BROADWAY—
YOUR WAY!

*With Special Material
for Working with Youth, Teens, the Disabled,
Challenged, Retired, and Computers*

David Young

**Routledge
New York & London**

Published in 1995 by
Routledge
29 West 35th Street
New York, NY 10001

Published in Great Britain by
Routledge
11 New Fetter Lane
London EC4P 4EE

Printed in the United States of America on acid-free paper.

Library of Congress Cataloging-in-Publication Data
Young, David.
     How to direct a musical Broadway—your way! : with special material for working with youth, teens, the disabled, challenged, retired, and computers / by David Young.
     p.   cm.
    Includes bibiographical references.
    ISBN 0-87830-052-X
    1. Musicals—Production and direction.   I. Title.
MT955.Y69   1994
792.6'0233—dc20

93-41612
CIP
MN

Acknowledgments

A big thank-you to Carole Brandt for her sage and generous advice; to Karen Berman (who kept the original diary), Jillian Poole, Gretchen Chellson, Lenny Granger, Mark Krikstan, Barbara Evans, Jerry Crawford, Harlene Marley, Charles Whitman, Tom Dunn, Violet Ketels, Jeanne Adams Wray, Winona Fletcher, Patricia Sternberg, Ron Willis, Willoughby, Charles Chestnut, and my wife Elizabeth, all for suggestions, additions, cuts, and shaping.

Finally to Lorene McClintock for her never-ending support and consciousness, and to all the students, teachers and colleagues who have shared and contributed so much, I'm eternally grateful!

SPECIAL THANKS TO DR. ANN RICHARDSON FOR HER WONDERFUL DIAGRAMS.

PHOTO CREDITS: *Fanny* and *Company* photos by Peter C. Piraneo, other from the archives of Pennsylvania State University, University of Missouri, Columbia, Mark Twain Masquers, Florida School of the Arts, Kennedy Center American College Theater Festival, and the author's personal collection. Sketches for *Fanny* set design by Dexter Dickinson.

Our production of *Fanny* was performed at the Little Theatre of Alexandria, a small, beautiful theatre in Alexandria, Virginia, a suburb of Washington, D.C. Its board of directors and support staff and photographers cannot be praised enough for their contribution to their community (and this book!).

Contents

Acknowledgments   v

Foreword
    Roger L. Stevens,
    Founding Chairman of the John F. Kennedy Center
    for the Performing Arts   xi

* Preface   xiii

Introduction   xv

1. BEFORE REHEARSALS BEGIN

The Guide   1
The Diary   3
Director's Book   3
Plot of the Musical *Fanny*   4
Checklist of Important Points in Each Musical Production   7
Script Analysis   7
*Setting the Style of Your Musical;   9
    Exploring the Musicals of the 1980s and 1990s   11
First Exercise   11
Collaborating with Designers, Crew, and Staff
    (first production meeting)   12
Specifics: costumes and wigs; sets (design and sketches);
    makeup; sound and lights; props and set dressing;
    stage manager; production book; rehearsal pianist   12
Musical Director and Choreographer   20
*The Director Who Stages His/Her Own Dances   21
For the Director Who Has Never Staged a Dance Number   22

2. *AUDITIONS AND CASTING

Sample Notice   25
Early Challenges   28

*Sections marked with asterisk * are for advanced work.

3. THE BEGINNING—First Rehearsals

Rehearsal Schedule   31
*Sample Autobiographies   34
Blocking (samples to use)   36
Staging the Musical Numbers (Diagrams Included)   39
Comparison of Similarities in Musical Numbers   42
Putting Together a Multicultural Musical Revue   43

4. *WORKING WITH SINGER/DANCERS ON ACTING— The Early Stages

Where Are We?   53
Listening: A Most Important Tool   55
*Characterization   56
Think Time for the Director   58
*Improvisation Theatre Games—To Help Strengthen
    and Enliven Rehearsals as the Pressure Begins   59

5. SPECIFIC CHALLENGES—Midway

Pulling the Musical Numbers Together   61
*Talking about Comedy   62
Farce—A Special Kind of Comedy   62
Stage Fights—How We Did Them!   63
*Accents   64
*Helping Singers to Age Realistically   64
Aging Americans and Theatre   65
More Production Meetings   66
Microphones   66
*Orchestra Rehearsals   66
Update and Relaxers   67
Run Through   68

6. *PACING, BLENDING, STREAMLINING

Pauses, How to Eliminate the Unwanted Ones   72
Special Rehearsal   73
Sorting Out   74
Plugging Along—Then Disaster   76
*Concentration—The Dustin Hoffman Story   77
*Videotaping Could Help   79
Publicity and Photographs—Necessary Interruptions   80

7. **ONSTAGE—FINALLY**
    Lights/Sound, Dry Tech   81
    Rehearsals with Sets, Costumes, and Tech   82
    More Observations   83
    *Some Breakthroughs   83
    Fine-Tuning the Songs   85
    Last Dress Rehearsals—Progress   86
    *Staging the Curtain Calls   88
    Preview   88
    Opening Night   90
    *Evaluation   90

APPENDICES

I.   *Understanding and Directing Young People and Teens
         Dr. Xan S. Johnson,
         Director of Theatre for Youth at the University of Utah   93

II. *Concerning Special Talents, or Whose Disability Is It Anyway?
         (How to Include and Direct People with Disabilities)
         J Ranelli,
         a director with a special talent for working with
         challenged populations   109

III. How to Stage Musical Numbers
         Dr. Nancy Vunovich
         musical theatre specialist   115

IV. The Choreographer/Director
         James M. Miller,
         Professor at the University of Missouri, Columbia   121

V.   *Computers for the Musical Theatre
         Dr. Roger Gross,
         University of Arkansas   135

GLOSSARY   149

RECOMMENDED READING/OTHER RESOURCES   153

ABOUT THE AUTHOR   155

INDEX   157

Roger L. Stevens,
founding
chairman,
John F. Kennedy
Center for
Performing Arts.

Foreword

January 1993

David Young has, for more than 15 years, been the Producing Director of the well-known American College Theatre Festival at the John F. Kennedy Center for the Performing Arts in Washington, D.C. In that capacity he has had the opportunity to visit almost 500 colleges nationally and internationally to see their theatre productions. David is himself a director and has acted and produced many plays and musicals. Because of that extensive experience and his work with community leaders, elementary and high school teachers, college theatre professors and students, David has a unique insight that few others in the theatre possess. He has now set forth his thoughts and ideas that he hopes will encourage those who wish to expand their horizons on how to stage and direct a musical.

David knows well the problems that can arise, and I think this work will be particularly valuable to anyone who sets out to do musical theatre. He explores the art and the craft of directing.

In my long association with David, I have always been most grateful for his energetic support and enthusiastic cooperation with all the ventures that have been undertaken annually at the Kennedy Center for the American College Theatre Festival.

Roger L. Stevens
Founding Chairman
The John F. Kennedy Center for the Performing Arts
Washington, D.C.

Act I of *Fanny*,
production
number,
full set.

David Young and
Luther Henderson,
composer, music
director, arranger
of Broadway's
Jelly's Last Jam.

Preface

If you have always wanted to direct a musical, or if you are searching for a new outlook for doing so, here is a way! I have written this book for you—it's a fast, practical, hands-on, do-it-yourself *text* and *guide*. From planning to casting, rehearsing to presentation, it shares the thoughts behind creative decisions, to ease any tension or fear you might have about directing a musical.

The book can also provide a shortcut for those who want to expand their horizons about how to put together a musical.* The aim is not just to recreate what was done on Broadway, but to help you put music, book, lyrics, and choreography together in your own way, while helping singer/actors to use the same *characterization* as they dance, speak, and sing. The voice and body quality of performers—when going from singing to speaking and vice versa—should remain consistent. Exercises throughout this book provide the means for you to aid your cast in doing this.

I have endeavored to make the process simple and not too cerebral.

Directing is problem-solving, planning, guiding, selecting, committing. If acting is doing, *directing* is bringing together, sharing, molding. The director's aim is helping the cast make contact with themselves, fellow performers, and the audience.

Included are parts of a *diary* that was kept while I directed the musical *Fanny*, by S. N. Berhman and Joshua Logan, music by Harold Rome, and a step-by-step *guide* to help you understand why decisions (even wrong ones) were made. I've spelled out specific problems in that production with the solu-

*Advanced work is noted this way in the table of contents.

tions found. Use the diary as a day-by-day trainer to enhance, stimulate, and broaden. The guide is a friend and mentor—a hands-on learning experience; the adventures I had, you will, too, as you direct your musical production.

Flow easily from the diary to the guide and vice versa as you would follow a road map. Note that the diary is in special type and marked with a sidebar for your convenience.

Sections that appear in a shaded block are provided as exercises. Please try them and put them to active use.

I suggest you read through the entire book, marking the exercises and noting the points that interest you. Then go back and work with each of these. Ideas will unfold as you progress through the book, and you will find some answers will come in the later parts of the book. Obviously, you cannot use all these ideas for any one production—they will change with the musical you choose and your own growth.

Be sure to look at: Appendix I on directing young people and teens by Dr. Xan S. Johnson, Appendix II on directing the disabled and challenged population by J Ranelli, and Appendix V by Dr. Roger Gross on including more of the ever-growing use of computers in musical theatre. They all have fine tips for *every* director.

When you've finished the book, watch for videotapes I'm developing to further bridge the gap between theory and practice.

Here is a note from a friend and colleague Barbara Evans to cheer you as you begin—

> It was heartwarming to read about other people's problems, actors who can't remember lines or blocking, technical headaches, the flubs and frustrations, but also the commitment, the drive and the energy, which reminded me once again of common goals, problem-solving techniques, and limitations, which we theatre folk face while we work toward achieving our best performances.

So let us explore the *craft* (and the *art*) of directing.

Introduction

Let's start by asking: "Why work in theatre arts?" I work in the theatre because I love it. Art gives value and order to *my* life; theatre then gives *form* to those feelings.

And the reason the subtitle is "Broadway, *Your* Way," is that you *don't* have to do your production like the Broadway production, and indeed you can't. You might as well face that fact and use what *you* have and who you are—and what your actor/singers, musicians, and designers have to share. If you combine all these elements, *you* can direct a musical, for the first time, or the 50th time, and your opening night is bound to be as interesting and creative, in its own right, as the original.

A number in the *Sound of Music* in the Broadway production and on the original cast tape or CD is a certain way because that's the staging of the first director—adjusted to the singing of Mary Martin and the company—but it isn't carved in stone. It needs to be adapted for your singer/actors. Our production of *Fanny* had to be different from what I saw in the Broadway production—300 seats versus 1300 to start—and we wouldn't have stars like Ezio Pinza, Walter Slezak, Florence Henderson or a chorus of 35—I would try to devise a well-rounded ensemble performance with less attention to large Broadway type production numbers and bumps and grinds.

Musicals provide the primary means by which the rest of the world perceives theatre in the U.S. All over the world Americans are famous for what is known as "musical comedy." (I prefer the term "musical theatre," as it gives a truer name and value to what we do.)

Musical theatre is a synthesis of people and art forms that are interwoven and blended together. As you know, in theatre you have a playwright, director, actors, designers, and crew who work together. In a musical theatre production, you have those same people and, in addition, a music director, choreographer, chorus, and orchestra.

Each musical, each production, is different—yet they all have many of the same pit- (and prat-!) falls. You won't find all of them in each musical you direct. The checklist and the patterns overlap (see page 7). If you are aware of the problems that *may* appear, you will be prepared to deal with them.

As we journey together, I will share my thoughts and passion about theatre; yet please bear in mind that there is always something more to do, learn, and explore. The real height of competition is not competing against someone else, but reaching within for the depths of your own capabilities. Failures are opportunities to learn and grow.

I'd like to share what the late Brooks Atkinson, critic emeritus of the *New York Times*, wrote many years ago that touched my heart:

> Theater civilizes, encourages beauty and dreaming. Theater almost always begins with a vision and ends in a performance. It makes strangers in the audience into a community of believers. Isn't that why most of us are in the theater? Art brings people together in a common emotional experience, sometimes even an intellectual one. Without the arts we are not fully alive.

And now please absorb and use this definition of what a director does in each of your productions.

> One of my oldest and wisest colleagues once said a director must be a traffic cop, tourist guide, choreographer, lion tamer, trial lawyer, magician, psychiatrist, babysitter, and con man. Not necessarily in alphabetical order. (Alan Schneider quote from a workshop I attended in the 1980's.)

Take this literally and you will see clearly that you do need to be a traffic cop when you are blocking a scene, a lion tamer when the going gets tough, and while the term "con man" might not be the polite word to use, I mean it in the sense of Harold Hill in *Music Man,* not in the sense of trickery. Directing is like climbing a mountain—sometimes it's rough, but when it is accomplished well, it's worth the extra effort.

David Young with a fellow teacher and a student.

Over the last 15 years, many have asked how to use the Stanislavski method in directing a musical. I use Stanislavski's methods for staging *the songs* as well as with the book and *in the choreography*. Examples follow.

> Near the turn of the nineteenth century, the Russian actor and director Konstantin Stanislavski developed a thorough system of actor training. After Stanislavski's death, his protege, Yvegeny Vakhtangov, refined and completed the system. Stanislavski dedicated himself to the central problem of stimulating the actor's creativity. He emphasized the use of observation, imagination, intuition, affective memory (sensory and emotional recall), combined with intensive vocal and physical study.
>
> —Dr. Jerry Crawford, *Acting in Person and in Style*

I always approach a musical from the center or spine, although the stylistic demands may seem different—find the inner life. With *West Side Story* a special problem existed with the original and continues to this day. Everyone tends to think of that musical as a success and believe that its success rides on the dancing. In fact, the

success rides on how well the singers can create believable roles and make connections which are not on the surface of the script. Great acting and coaching are required to make that musical successful—just great dancing or singing will *not* get the job done.
>   —Gerald Freedman, director,
>   whose credits include, among others, *West Side Story*
>   and *Robber Bridegroom* on Broadway

As a start, determine what is *central* or at the *heart* of your production. You, as a director, need to discover the inside of the plot, just as actors and singers must discover what their characterizations are and what their characters think and feel underneath what they say and sing.

[Characterization: The endowment of a role with particular traits and behavioral patterns belonging specifically to the character the actor imagines, creating a past that belongs to the character.] Even the simplest musicals have a central core. Musicals, like *Carousel* and *My Fair Lady,* have classic themes at their roots.

Remember, there is nothing like a musical—it's magical!

1

Before Rehearsals Begin

The Guide

Selection is central to a successful musical production. Choose the one for your group based on what talent you have. Ask yourself: 1) Can we cast it? 2) Can the group produce it? 3) Does it have audience and box office appeal? *Fanny* was selected because we said yes to most of those criteria.

Obviously, you won't choose a musical with demanding dance sequences if you haven't dancers. If you're in an area in which virtually no one can do a British accent, you probably don't want to do a British musical (unless you can find someone who can coach the cast). If you only have a group of six to eight people, don't attempt a musical that calls for a large chorus.

There are any number of musicals to do. Here are sample musical categories. I've also listed the names of the major licensing agencies that own the rights to musicals—they will be happy to send you catalogues. Ask for a perusal copy—go over the libretto and music, and if possible, find the original cast tape or CD. There are stores in many large cities that specialize in selling out-of-print material. That way you can actually hear what the music sounded like. Review the score and play it over and over—to be sure that the music inspires you or touches your heart or funny bone.

Organize your rehearsal time early. You can over-rehearse some parts to the detriment of others. When I've staged all the musical numbers, I quite often rehearse Act II first to equalize the energy and time spent working on each.

Sample Musical Categories

1. Book shows: *City of Angels, Cabaret, Oklahoma!*
2. Dance shows: *Cats, 42nd Street, Grand Hotel*
3. Ensemble shows: *Godspell, Aspects of Love, You're a Good Man, Charlie Brown*
4. Revues: *Side by Side by Sondheim, Jacques Brel Is Alive and Well and Living in Paris, Lend an Ear*
5. Operettas: *Desert Song, The Mikado, Rose Marie*
6. Cabaret theatre: *Pump Boys and Dinettes, Song of Singapore, Forever Plaid*
7. A vehicle for a major star: *Mame, Fiddler on the Roof, Annie Get Your Gun*
8. Musicals that are mostly music: *Les Misérables, Phantom of the Opera, Miss Saigon*

Licensing Agencies (partial listing)

Samuel French, Inc., 45 West 25th Street, New York, NY 10010 (212) 206-8990

Music Theatre International, 545 Avenue of the Americas, Eighth Floor, New York, NY 10018, (212) 868-6668

Rodgers and Hammerstein Library, 1633 Broadway, Suite 3801, New York, NY 10019, (212) 541-6600

Tams-Whitmark, Music Library, 560 Lexington Avenue, New York, NY 10022, (212) 688-2525

Dramatic Publishing Company, 311 Washington St., P.O. Box 109, Woodstock, IL 60098 (junior and high school market), (815) 338-7170

Remember, there are four main sections to any musical: 1) lead songs, 2) company songs, 3) dialogue and lyrics, and 4) dances. Be sure each gets enough rehearsal (if that's ever possible).

A musical should move with more energy than a play—the opening number and first-act finale and second-act conclusion are the most important from the audience's point of view. From the first rise of the curtain until it descends at the end of Act II—try never to let the action stop or the lights go to black. Certainly, when a blackout is necessary, music can come in so the audience doesn't get restless.

One important thing to keep in mind is that a musical should never look like work on opening night.

The Diary

Director's Book

In doing my pre-planning work, I assembled my Director's Book. It had both the libretto (also referred to as book), the score, and contained all recommendations for designers and crews, my blocking of each page of dialogue and musical number, in addition to notes to myself on the production's look and style. Both acts were broken down into sections as to what would be worked on at each rehearsal.

For all of the musical numbers, I marked the places in my Director's Book where every character was standing and had his/her exit. Having this overall plan makes it easier to fit songs and dances and book together seamlessly.

Here is a sample page of musical numbers in *Fanny* from my Director's Book—and how my thinking on them started.

SOLOS

"Never too Late"—Simple. Just *Panisse* showing off and the company enjoying him.

"Welcome Home"—Twilight. *Cesar* alone, soaking up the atmosphere of the French town.

"To My Wife"—A serious change for *Panisse*; standing still; we're seeing the progression from Act I to Act II.

"Love Is a Very Light Thing"—*Cesar*, like Panisse, a different man in Act II, more mature.

DUO/TRIOS

"I Like You"—Simple father/son with the attention on the two men; played in their bar, which is their home.

"Fanny"—Romantic, sexy; in follow spots played downstage; the romantic number of the show.

"I Have To Tell You"—Passionate duet done on the stairs; this treatment will make it dramatic yet true to life.

"Fanny Reprise"—Trio; they are older, more serious, rather still.

---

4   *Before Rehearsals Begin*

CHORUS

"Restless Heart"—Opening of the show. Marius and ensemble making use of the fact that Marius is 17; it's all male so it can be quite physical with the men lifting him up, throwing him around. Young, athletic.

"Why Be Afraid"—A big group number; leads and all interchanging; will be worked by choreographer.

"Birthday Song"—Very simple, but beautiful song; chorus might sit on the edge of the stage and sing to the audience; chance to show off the ensemble with follow-spot on each face.

Twenty years ago, I started a career-long diary of interesting directing concepts and wonderful stagings that I have seen and enjoyed. I have it to refer to when I'm doing my own work, especially if I'm stuck for an idea. Borrow from the best. When you see work by someone like Tommy Tune, we may not have that kind of talent, but there's nothing wrong with using one (or two) of his ideas or movements in our productions.

Plot of the Musical Fanny

To make it easier for you to follow the diary portions, *Fanny* is set in Marseilles in 1910, with Act II taking place 17 years later.

It is the tender story of a young French girl, Fanny, and her bittersweet affair with a restless young man, Marius. Fanny is the daughter of Honorine, a fishmonger, and Marius is the son of Cesar, the owner of a waterfront cafe.

Fanny has been in love with Marius for some time. Cesar expects Marius to take over the family business one day, but the boy wants to go to sea. An old codger, "The Admiral," influences Marius to sign on secretly with a ship's crew. Marius confides his plans to Fanny, who, heartbroken, surrenders herself to him. He goes off to sea, unknowingly leaving her pregnant.

A wealthy sailmaker, Panisse (who is about the same age as Marius's father) has recently become a widower. He offers to marry Fanny and adopt her child. Although Fanny does not love Panisse, she accepts his proposal rather than suffer the disgrace of bearing an illegitimate child.

Grease at the Florida School of the Arts, Palatka. Dr. David Humphrey, Dean. Directed by the author.

In Act II Fanny has had her son and Panisse is credited with being the father; they lead a normal and fairly happy married life. The son is named Cesario.

Just as all seems to be well, Marius returns to visit (unhappily, on Cesario's sixteenth birthday). When Marius finds out the truth, he is overwhelmed and wants to claim his son.

The good sense of Fanny, Marius's father, and Fanny's mother prevails, and they convince him to return to the sea, after a love song, of course. In a bittersweet finale, Panisse dies, leaving everything to Fanny and Cesario.

Subplot

The musical has a subplot involving Cesar and Panisse's old buddies Brun and Escartifique; this subordinate story provides comic relief similar to the ones in such operettas as *The Merry Widow* and *The Desert Song*.

Several months before I began casting, I went to see half a dozen musicals and made notes of interesting ideas I might use to expand my planning. For instance—bringing some of the musicians onstage for the songs, using tambourines, a maypole, kneeling for the songs using big pillows, using high stools or a ladder—all of these added to my original thoughts. I felt one or two of them might give our production a more diversified and interesting look and feeling. I actually used a maypole in one song as it fit my needs—and I thanked the director I borrowed it from. She said she had borrowed the idea from another director's production of a different musical!

There is an old French movie of *Fanny* (in black and white), as well as the 1960's Hollywood technicolor version starring Leslie Caron. I went to see both films on video and later took the cast and crew so they, too, had this information. It was fascinating for us all to see what the time period looked like. My feeling was that Marius and Fanny, the romantic leads, who are 17 the first time we meet them, must progress to mid-thirties in the second act. I'd have to cast carefully to find people in that mid-age level who could sing yet act both ages realistically.

The music director suggested I find a Fanny who could use a soprano voice for Act I and add her chest voice for Act II, and for the role of Marius we find a tenor with some baritone range (bari-tenor). This would help to make the aging sound natural.

As I mentioned, one of the first things I did was listen to the music—it gave tips and told what to do with the staging. What does the lyric say? How does each song advance the plot? If there were no music attached, what would the movements (blocking) be in naturalistic terms? Then, as I listened to the music again and again, it led my body to go where and when an actor/singer might move; where the actress/dancer should raise her arm; when the ensemble should put their hands on their hips; where they might kneel; when they would all move to the left or downstage. Does it seem comfortable? Can the cast sing and still do this? (I usually start with far too many movements. So I trim, trim.) Movement should be motivated by the emotions of the words and/or by the rhythm of the song. Motivation is plausible behavior for a given character.

Try to add touches of reality to each number—for instance, in *Fanny* we used fishnets, a ladder, barrels, and a bed; staging one number over the bed, through the nets, up and down the ladder, and around the barrels was fun and logical.

Dream of using some of the wonderful "theatrical" effects that go with musicals: a follow spot, moonlight, stars blinking, or black light, which gives an ultraviolet quality to a number.

Envision what the number will look like at the opening. For instance, if the scene takes place in the evening (blue light), the movement may be softer than if in peppy, bright sunlight; if it's in the corner of the set rather than across the entire stage, then it might have to have less movement—more with arms and torso, not as much with the feet.

■ Here is a:

Checklist of Important Points in Each Production

1. Pre-plan *everything*.
2. Ask for one extra week of rehearsals so you can use the exercises in this book. Three or five extra rehearsals over the rehearsal period can be lifesavers.
3. Find a stage manager who is willing and able to unburden the director of detail work.
4. Hire a choreographer and musical director who work cooperatively *with* the director for efficient, creative use of the rehearsal time, by having some of the cast work with the musical director while director works with the others and the choreographer works with the dancers.
5. Be sure your original set and costume designs are thought out so that changes are fast and easy. Have as few pauses and blackouts as possible and if you do have them, be sure they are covered by music.
6. Work out all light changes and use lights early enough (one week before tech week) so the last three or four rehearsals aren't just tech.

Script Analysis

When I start my script analysis, I try to define (and write down) what my concept is, what the center or action of the musical is. And I try, as mentioned earlier, to discover the *inside* of the book and lyrics—*the subtext*—rather than just the surface. (See also page 50 on subtext for singer/dancer/actors by Lee Strasberg.) Subtext is a term central to the Stanislavski system and method according to Dr. Larry Clark in *Acting Is Believing,* Holt Rinehart, Winston, 1986. It refers to the meaning underlying the dialogue and stage directions. Subtext may include imagined autobiographical material about a character, provided that it is clearly related to the text and not merely arbitrary. I like to find out what is going on behind the words and lyrics—what's happening on a gut level. I find the heart of each character as I get to know the songs. And if a character is *saying* one thing yet meaning something else, then I must help the actor/singers to experience the motivation that is causing the emotions and the dialogue.

A good example of this is a story, supposedly about movie star Joan Crawford, who, as you know, worked in film musicals and dramas. She had a favorite scene, one in which she's saying goodbye to her lover on the phone, telling him it's okay and that he should go off with a younger woman. Of course, inside she's crying and hysterical, yet though her heart is breaking, she is saying and doing the right thing. You see that even though she's saying "Go away with her, it's okay" (text), in her heart she's hurting (subtext).

Explore each character's feelings and share them with your company, and then help the cast to experience *both*, the inner and the outer of the character's emotions, as they *sing* and speak.

> In preparation for sharing with the *Fanny* cast, I tried to write down what I felt the author's point of view was, in three to five sentences. I started with two full pages about this, but then zeroed in on five lines so as to be specific.
>
> I analyzed the strengths and the weaknesses of our musical so as to counteract the weaknesses and support all the strengths.
>
> The weaknesses of *Fanny*, as explored, are 1) that the slightly saccharine, old-fashioned nature of the book must be very truthfully and realistically acted, 2) songs that are partly operetta-ish should be sung with the passion and naturalism of Rodgers & Hammerstein (if the audience is to have the in-depth experience wanted). I would counterbalance this by casting carefully and not allowing any musical comedy cuteness to surface. As always, *25 percent of any successful production is inspired casting.*
>
> The strengths are 1) that the score is very beautiful, and 2) I felt this was the right time to do a musical in which the book indicates goodness wins and honor should be cherished (STILL DO!).

Here are nine points I work out before rehearsing any musical production.

1. What is the musical about (in four to six lines)?
2. What is the action before the musical begins?
3. Whose musical is it? (In this case it was Fanny's—but actually the two fathers are central to the story.)
4. What is the main theme of the script?
5. What are the environments of this musical?
6. Chart the structure of this production and justify my concept.
7. Find the character line for each person; the through lines; the plot lines.
8. What is each song's goal and how does it fit into the overall production? Find the important beats (book and lyrics) and, with the cast, determine each character's objectives for each unit.
9. What will be the major problems—how will I work them out?

Setting the Style of Your Musical

The style of a musical is determined by action that comes out of the *needs* of the characters, not from a director superimposing it. Webster defines *style* as "a distinctive manner of expression or particular technique by which something is done, created, or performed"—a kind of appearance, of character, and action. "Making the transformation from everyday behavior to the goals of the character," as Robert Cohen defines it in *Acting Power,* Mayfield Publishing, 1978.

The way people lived tells you a lot. For instance, in the early part of this century European society frowned upon premarital sex for females. Our ingenue, Fanny, is not over-coy, she's just behaving the way she perceives that young women should behave in 1910.

In the Victorian era people read by gaslight and rode in horse-drawn carriages; their clothing was tight and heavy. This dictated how they moved and helped shape what they were. As director, I hoped to help the cast bring a relaxed, easy atmosphere into this story so audiences would sense it's early in the 20th century and not the more frantic, hedonistic lifestyle of today. The way people of each period lived and thought is how style is determined. *Life dictates style.*

I went to the library to look at photographs of clothes and furniture (circa 1910); also, I was asking myself what people's mental states were, what the current events and the major news stories of the time were. (Newspapers and magazines from the period gave me great ideas.) I brought much of this to share with the cast early in rehearsals.

So, setting style is a matter of knowledge of the period and of what happened to the people in that time.

The style of our production of *Fanny* would be similar to Rodgers and Hammerstein in their *Carousel* period: as life-like as possible. Yet there would be no Agnes de Mille dream choreography.

Another type of style is that of the composer and is a consideration when directing singers to work on a specific composer's work—Sondheim, Porter, Weber, Rodgers and Hammerstein. Each has his own style—this is a different consideration completely from what we have been discussing about period style. To help make this clear here is a quote from David Craig in *On Singing Onstage,* McGraw Hill, 1989:

> It is also of interest to the actor/singer to learn that each composer "speaks" music with different accents, personal and distinctive, in

Cast and crew of *Fanny*.

much the same manner that playwrights do. The actor does not play Odets as he plays Sheridan, Shakespeare as he would Chekhov, or Pirandello as he would Neil Simon. His task, among many, is to duplicate the tonality of the play. It is no less so when he sings. Just as, in more serious (appalling word!) music, Mozart is not interpreted in the manner of Tchaikovsky, Chopin as Beethoven, or Stravinsky as Strauss, theatre-music composers leave their signatures on everything they write. Among the more "standard" composers, Gershwin, Rodgers (more with Hart than with Hammerstein), Porter (in his more playful moods), Berlin, early Lane, and Loesser wrote and write most often for performers rather than singers. The actor can feel comfortable singing their songs with a minimum of strain and overt display of vocal inadequacy. But Kern, Arlen, Loewe, Rodgers (in his operetta settings of some of Hammerstein's work), Bernstein, the more lavish Porter, Schwartz, and latter-day Lane are all distinctly more sumptuous melodists who require voices adequate enough to "sing" them as well as "play" them. This is, of course, a general observation. But if your singing is not of a high degree of musical splendor, pick up with care the work of these men. They are not the best of friends of actors whose voices are not their calling cards.

Exploring the Musicals of the 1980's and 1990's

Let's also explore the style of the so-called new type of musical of the 1980's and 1990's, many from Great Britain, such as *Les Misérables, Evita, Phantom of the Opera, Aspects of Love*; they are quasi-operatic—that is, almost exclusively music, with the book as well as songs set to music. Parts of the music are more melodic—they are the "song" part of the musical, and the other music is more "recitative"; in these the book or script is sung rather than spoken.

Exercise

In the case of these new musicals, having the actors *speak* the lyrics as an exercise in rehearsal is critical. Speaking and exploring the emotions of the lyrics will give the singers energy, understanding, and continuity when they return to singing.

Take a page of music and lyrics and ask your actors to *say* the lyrics (and *not sing*), to explore those words and the feeling behind them. You will find they begin to feel what is underneath or behind the words. Then ask them to put the music back in (slowly—1/2 spoken and 1/2 sung) and then to rediscover those feelings as they sing entirely.

Work with these new musicals exactly the same way you would with *Crazy for You, City of Angels, Company, South Pacific,* or *Anything Goes*—*there is no real difference*—except that book and music are both sung. Much of what we're exploring in this quest is that book, lyrics, and music are all one—in these new musicals the creators have, in a sense, done part of the work for us.

Please note: THESE NEW MUSICALS DO TAKE ABOUT *20 PERCENT MORE* REHEARSAL TIME because of the huge amount of music.

Collaborating with Designers, Crew and Staff

Our first production meeting was called to introduce all of the design and crew chiefs to one another, and to explore further the concept of the production. Each had an important part to play in the creation of the final product. Therefore, we would all need to be as one in our vision. We agreed to meet *once a week* for the *balance* of *rehearsals*. I began by saying that I felt that our production of *Fanny* should be a real story with a solid, colorful, three-dimensional look—a play that happens to have music. I was striving at this meeting, and as I had at the many pre-production meetings, to allow my collaborators' ideas to enlarge my production ideas.

Specifics

This information will be most helpful in working creatively with your Production Staff. Most of these notes were made after our first production meeting, before rehearsals began.

Costumes and Wigs

The costume designer wanted the clothes to be as realistic as possible, true to the period (1910–27) and the rural French working class, and they would be designed to not look too clean or pretty. She mentioned aprons, kerchiefs, spats, bow ties, pointed shoes, cummerbunds, and lots of color (partly gleaned from seeing the movie of *Fanny*). We envisioned each chorus member to be a specific character—not just a dancer or singer, but a policeman, washerwoman, etc.—so each would need attire reflecting the character's identity.

The character of Fanny is central throughout. A large part of the costume budget would go into her clothes, as she embodies the different moods and time changes of the musical. To help her age from 17 to mid-thirties during the show would require several wigs (we decided during Hell Week not to use them because they looked fake). The designer wanted Fanny's wedding dress to be

Carnival,
**University
of Florida,
Dr. Judith
Williams,
chair.**

very simple and planned the wedding for the morning—yet this did not deter
her from dressing the men in tails, thus allowing them to display their ignorance
of social etiquette.

Make a list of which characters will have quick changes and plan that those
costumes will be ready first for the cast to use early in rehearsal. (Note—an
alternative to this plan, if the costume cannot be available, is for the actor/
singer to practice the quick change by getting out of his/her own rehearsal
clothes and back into them again, simulating what will actually happen.) If
these fast changes are not worked out ahead of time, final rehearsals can be
ruined because of the pressure of making them.

Getting the feeling early in rehearsals (second week) of the shoes worn by
their characters will also increase the cast's ability to move freely. Rehearsal
skirts were used even in our first blocking rehearsals. The company's mea-
surements should be taken at the second music rehearsal, and set a date for
the costume parade (see glossary).

Plot of First Costume Ideas

Act-Scene	Fanny	Marius	Cesar	Panisse
1-1	Very young	Very young	Day clothes	Day clothes
1-3	Shawl	Jacket, cap	Hat	
1-5	Dress (nice)		Jacket off	Jacket off
1-6	Apron			
1-7	Skirt/blouse		2nd suit	2nd suit
1-8	Wedding dress		Tails	Tails
1-9			Night shirt	Night shirt and robe
2-1	Kerchief, mature dress			
2-2	Elegant day dress	Sailor white, moustache	Older person's suit, cane	Mature person's tweed suit, flower
2-3		Knickers	Knickers	Knickers
2-4	Older, in an elegant dress		Jacket	Shirt, slacks jacket
2-6		(little potbelly?)		
2-7	Mature dress		Shirt, sweater	Night shirt

Act/Scene	Honorine	Escartifique/ Brun	Chorus	Cesario
1-1	Work clothes	Day clothes	Day clothes	
1-6	Apron			
1-8	Dress, wedding			
1-9	Expensive-looking dress, but vulgar		Night clothes, PJs, etc.	
2-1	Older, rich, splashy	Older, funny tie, etc.	Older	
2-2	New (style)			
2-4	Older			Knickers
2-5			Circus party	
2-6				Long pants
2-7	Calm, nice dress		Same	

Sketch of set
for *Fanny*,
Act I.

Sets

The first look at the set model for Act I, though different from my original
thoughts, was exciting.

Viewing it from afar, below, above, and from audience level, with an objective
eye, moving the set pieces as if they were parts of a doll's house, we felt the set
met the functional and aesthetic requirements necessary to both contain and free
the action.

At stage right (SR) sat the "Bar de la Marine," with a brightly striped awning
and a window cutout behind which Cesar would tend bar. Stage left (SL), forming
a "V" with the bar, stood the storefront labeled "Panisse," behind which we
would find Panisse and his sails. Upstage left and right (UL & R) sat a high,
stacked block of dockside lumber, and, behind it, fishnets and rope ladders to
the ceiling.

Behind these *movable* set pieces was a beautiful painted backdrop of the sea, sky,
and other storefronts within the little village.

In our budget planning, it appeared that for the sake of cost (and convenience), it
might be possible in Act II to use a portion of wall and stairway from the set of
the show preceding ours. The set designer wanted a very solid feeling for Act II,
as it was Panisse and Fanny's new, expensive home. We decided to use the left

Fanny, Act II.

half of the previous production's set, and their large, solid stair unit which the designer put on rollers. By swinging the set piece around and bringing in the new stairs at an angle, there was a spacious, different look at minimal cost.

Panisse's house would be filled with warm colors because of his loving persona, the decor showing evidence of money, but not necessarily money tastefully spent. It would be pre–Art Deco, with peacock feathers and frou-frou.

We had talked of easing the work of the set crew by using drops so the set could be changed quickly behind them. When a drop went up, there would be another set behind it. But the drop design proved too flimsy for what was needed. The designer also toyed at one time with using slide projections—all were discarded early as too unrealistic for our production plan.

Originally, a third part to the set in Act I was envisioned—the fish stall where Fanny's mother, Honorine, works. But since there was no room for it onstage, we "cooked up" the idea of putting her *fish* stand on a bicycle so she could ride it in and out. She was a rather large lady, and we all thought it would be a true (and comic) addition to the production and would uncrowd our stage. She came and went with her own set piece on the bike.

Makeup

Finding the right makeup person is critical for any production. Seek the right artist and communicate *exactly* what you want, so you won't find your leading man made up to look like he's just stepped out of a second-rate touring show—but rather, that he looks like the robust fisherman you have envisioned.

Usually I ask that the leads do their own makeup, in consultation with the makeup artist, and that the inexperienced cast members let the makeup artist design their makeup and demonstrate *how* they can eventually do it for themselves.

> Our makeup designer came in early (second week), so he could get a good look at the cast and explore; if the young woman playing one of the leads had a complexion problem, then she might need a special makeup to give her that "young glow," or if one of the male leads who was a bit chubby, he might need his cheeks rounded with beard liner to make him look tougher and thinner.

> Of course, eventually you must see the makeup under the stage lights, because it looks one way in the rehearsal space or dressing room and another onstage. For instance, as soon as you see the makeup under blue lights or a purple follow spot, you quickly notice it changes the lipstick and rouge color.

> Our makeup artist helped the cast visualize their physical look early in rehearsal. Seeing their *age* makeup in the mirror helped our two young leads to get more of the feeling and look as to how they must age for Act II.

Sound and Lights

> At our first discussion (on the telephone) I asked the sound designer to think in terms of seagulls, buoy bells, crickets, and water sounds, to help give a natural background sound to the production. We agreed this would help give the musical a realistic and solid feeling.

> The lighting designer and I had talked through the entire show scene by scene. He suggested a very naturalistic look for book sections and special highlights for songs, except for the major love song ("Fanny") and dances, for which we would use two follow spots to heighten the audience reaction.

I suggested that we move up our first lighting tech by a week, so that the first onstage light rehearsals would be less hectic. (In the past I've found that a major hurdle has been that I spend much of the last three or four rehearsals working with the lighting designer, adjusting the light intensity, rather than directing the cast.)

And yes, the opening number of the show would require a fog machine—to help give the atmosphere, look, and mood of a waterfront.

Props and Set Dressing

Before our first production meeting I had worked with the set designer and set dresser (person who finds furniture, drapes, rugs, etc.), thinking out possible furniture arrangements. They chose just enough furniture to create the atmosphere needed yet leave room for dances and easy furniture changes. (The set designer and stage manager had taped the shape of the set out on the stage floor 48 hours before we went into rehearsal so I could walk and move around on it to make sure my blocking ideas worked.)

The property master had made a list of all props. The list included pictures cut from magazines to show the crew what was needed. This specificity saved time and *money*.

Rehearsal props (substitute props used to save wear and tear on performance props) were used after the first week of rehearsals.

Stage Manager

Choosing the right stage manager (SM) can make the difference between a productive rehearsal period and a tense one. I look for a solid, down-to-earth, patient, sympathetic person who will be my liaison with the cast and crew. Experience is of course necessary, but the right human being is truly the key.

The SM and I went over all the scenes and musical numbers, listing which singer/actors were in each. This way, when we rehearsed, we could excuse people when they were no longer needed and not waste their time and energy. We talked through the script, scene by scene, so he knew my thoughts. Of course, much would change in the rehearsal process.

For his Production Book (see next section), the SM had made a large libretto and music book in which to note all of the blocking. Eventually he would add in the

Inexpensive, imaginative set design. University of Florida, Dr. Judith Williams, chair.

sound and light cues, warning cues for the actors, and the scene changes. He would organize each scene change, including furniture, and eventually the changes would be rehearsed—first in the light, then in dark.

Since the SM is the boss once you open, calling all the cues, giving notes, and looking after the entire production, I felt he would need to know my innermost plans and thoughts for our musical.

Production Book

The stage manager made a Production Book (not to be confused with the director's book—see page 3) by cutting out the actual script and pasting each page onto an 8 1/2 x 11-inch sheet to provide room for notes and recording the blocking, also for marking sound cues in one color, lighting cues in another. The book would be used during the actual run of the show, and cues would be easy to follow. He left room for diagrams, a place for notes about special props and other information that might be needed during technical rehearsals, and space for warning cues to actors for upcoming scenes and to crews for set changes.

A Production Book is an important guide that enables the SM and the company to keep the show on target—so that a week after the opening, the audience will see the same musical that you directed.

Rehearsal Pianist

The rehearsal pianist is central to the progress of your production. It is preferable that the rehearsal pianist be a musician who will have the feeling for what you and the musical director are trying to accomplish. Since your musical director can't be at every rehearsal, the rehearsal pianist must be in communication with the music director and vice versa, so they can relate the changes that are made each day.

I try to hire a rehearsal pianist who is someone I know of or have worked with before, who is flexible and able to bend with the flow. This person may very well be the music director for one of my next productions.

Musical Director and Choreographer

The work of our musical director was to plan and organize the music rehearsals, arrange for a rehearsal pianist, teach the cast the music, and, of course, to conduct and play in the small orchestra (for many productions, two pianos and drums work fine).

Previously the musical director had played all of the incidental music (music used in score for characterization enhancement or to bridge scene changes), so I could get the sound and feel of it. We saved some for emergency delays in set changes, though usually the music director will just repeat what was just played in those cases.

The musical numbers were organized into those for principals and those for ensemble. The ensemble members were rehearsed first at music rehearsals, and then excused. Waiting is counterproductive. This also enabled the principals to get used to working together and to know one another early in the process.

The music director assured me that the orchestra (only five pieces: mandolin, bass, drum, accordion, and piano) would create an authentic turn-of-the-century French sound and feeling. We had already penciled in early orchestra rehearsals so the orchestra would have one rehearsal at least two weeks before opening, to get used to the singers and vice versa. I had, of course, deferred to the musical director's knowledge in choosing the musicians.

The choreographer would teach the dancers to move, design all the dances, and supervise all of the general movement for the group numbers. We had previously worked out who would stage each of the musical numbers, including the ones we would work on together Depending on your collaboration, it is not unusual for the director to stage solos, duos and small group numbers and the choreographer (in collaboration with the director) to stage the large ensemble numbers. In ensemble numbers, in this case, I worked with the principals, the choreographer with ensemble This arrangement is determined on basis of the strengths and preferences of the creative team.

Time was scheduled for the choreographer and the dancers to go over the plan and composition of each dance and to confirm the dance rehearsal schedule, as they would rehearse in another space. We also scheduled time for the choreographer to meet with the principals to work them into the ensemble dance numbers.

Those who are less experienced with dance will find that the choreographer uses the same approach as a director or author—basing his/her composition on the dramatic situation (and the talents of the cast members). Many choreographers listen to the music and write a scenario (specifics in the next sections).

Dance routines can only be learned by rote, and then repeated (and repeated). There is no other way—repetition leads to polishing.

Let the performers look their best even if you must simplify your work to a two-step and swaying. A relaxed dancer looks better because he/she is confident and having fun. Complicated steps poorly executed help no one.

You will not always have the creative production team I was lucky to have, so it will sometimes take a certain amount of cajoling, nagging, training, and feeding to get the results you need.

The Director Who Stages His/Her Own Dances

Jim Miller is a director/choreographer I had the pleasure of working with. (He is an instructor at the University of Missouri—Columbia.) Jim's shows always look beautiful and seem so easily shaped. During our talks he said, "Staging the musical numbers and choreography, for me, is like sculpting—I enjoy moving the actors around much the same as a sculptor likes moving clay around."

This director had never thought of it that way, because choreography is not something I do easily. But if you think about it in those terms and work out some simple choreography, or "sculpting," for your musical numbers, it is helpful and eases your task of placing the cast and creating the steps. (Obviously, the "sculpture" will have to have feet, and the feet

Dance— final dress rehearsal.

will have to move.) What an enlightening observation Professor Miller had to share.

(See Appendix IV by him for additional ideas for staging musical numbers than the ones I write of in the next chapters.)

For the Director Who Has Never Staged a Dance

Dance is choreographed with exactly the same approach as blocking, depending on the dramatic situation, intent, and characters at that particular moment, according to Carveth Osterhaus, director and choreographer for the Oklahoma City University Musical Theatre program. "Sit down, listen to that music, and write a scenario. Then, divide up the music and decide how many people exactly are on the stage, and for how many counts they'll be doing something."

Dance, from the simple to the most complex, is all choreographed in this manner. Even Balanchine did his homework first, sitting there with a tape recorder and a score—and listing side by side with the score:

A) a scenario

B) particular step patterns and

C) stage positions for each section of 8 beats for sub-group of players or dancers.

Exercise (by C. Osterhaus)

Take ten people. Divide them into groups, say two groups of 3 and two groups of 2. Work in floor patterns, as if looking down on the stage or a floorplan. Each small group will be working in a particular section of the stage. The music is divided by beats into patterns of 8 counts, and a series of different rhythms or patterns of counting are developed to those 8 counts: one, two, three . . . , or one and two and three . . . , or one, (pause), three, four . . . , and the like. Each small group is working with a varied pattern of the 8 count. First the dancers clap the rhythm in order to learn it. Then they tap it out with their feet while still seated. Finally, they get up and march in place to the rhythm. All of dancing boils down to simple marching in terms of footwork, left-right-left-right stepping in the rhythm pattern of the 8 counts. Then the stepping pattern can be varied by either doing it in place, or moving forward and backward, or by moving to the left or the right.

Do *not* repeat the same step, even with simple movement variations, for more than 32 counts (four repetitions of the 8 count pattern). Therefore, most numbers would require about three entirely different step-pattern routines, each covering 32 counts. Careful pre-planning is the key to success. The director needs to count out the music and write down the number of 8 count rhythm sections. Then, plan different variations of the 8 pattern for each small group, as well as the particular area of the stage each will occupy. A useful variation is to have small groups exchange areas of the stage at some point during the number.

Auditions and Casting

Fanny Casting Notice

Auditions for the musical production, *Fanny,* will be held Saturday at 2 p.m. and Sunday at 7:30 p.m. David Young will direct. He is looking for the following to audition:

2 character actors, 40–50, must be experienced singers and actors

1 leading man, 25–30, tenor

1 leading lady, 25–30, soprano

1 character actress, 45, comedienne, singing optional

1 young boy, 12–15, must sing and act well

2 character actors, 35–50, must act well, singing optional

3 male dancers who can play small parts

3 female dancers who can play small parts

5 male singers, 16–60, who can play several parts

5 female dancer/singers, 16–60, who can play several parts

1 belly dancer

1 juggler

Those auditioning should come prepared with a theatrical song to demonstrate vocal range. Readings will be assigned from the script. Dress so you can move freely.

On our first of two audition days, the assistant director, musical director, choreographer, and I assembled in the rehearsal room before the auditioners arrived. I had chosen several pages from the script for the readings. They were posted by entrance way for all to see. In the front hall of the theatre the assistant stage manager sat at a table, showing each prospective cast member a rehearsal schedule and a descriptive list of characters in the play as well as handing out an audition form that stipulated the following:

1) List any conflicts on the form and plan to be at all other rehearsals needed, without exception.

2) All parts are open, and you may request reading for any part.

3) Callbacks will be held on Monday at 7 p.m.

4) The director has the right to replace or exchange actors during rehearsals, if necessary.

Each was then asked to complete the form, and attach a resume; lacking the latter, prospective cast members were asked for the following:

1) Name, age range

2) Height, weight, color of hair and eyes

3) Previous theatrical experience

4) Special talents

5) Character he/she prefers to audition for (if any)

6) Voice range

7) Dance or movement experience

Once this process was completed, the actor/singer/dancers were escorted upstairs, where each sat for an instant Polaroid photograph. We shot in groups of three or four, then cut the photos up and attached individual faces to their resume/audition sheet, in order to save money on film. (We also made sure to *date* the photographs—and to keep them on file for future reference.) They were then called into the tryout room in groups of five or six.

I stepped forward for a quick tete-a-tete with each group, trying to get acquainted before the formal audition process began. I handed out this quote from Colleen Dewhurst in the *New York Times* to help them understand how I feel about the theatre and what I would expect from them if cast:

"When I started in the theatre—just like a kid—it was, I like the theatre. Then it was, I love the theatre. Now it's more than that. I

David Young, center, acting in *Noises Off,* Pennsylvania Center Stage, Carole Brandt, artistic director.

don't even know myself anymore. I think that theatre is a purification for actors and for the audience. It's telling the audience, almost subliminally, where you and they are at this time."

During these auditions I used two actor/readers (one male and one female) to help fill in parts when the auditioners didn't fit the bill. Those readers would *not* be in the production.

Bringing in small groups allowed me to see how the auditioners relate as individuals and in a group experience. After a *brief* chat, each performer was asked to sing, and then they were given one or two pages of dialogue to read. For some I asked for changes in what they were doing—to see how flexible they might be.

When I ran late (as I always seem to do after the second hour), I popped into the waiting room and informed those who were there that I was still alive and hadn't forgotten them. I asked that please, no one leave unless I was told about it or he or she made an appointment to return. (I was beginning to establish the director/actor relationship immediately.)

Then the choreographer taught each group a short routine consisting of four basic steps. We looked for limberness, flexibility, competence in following directions, memory of the steps, coordination, and grace.

A new colleague suggested I use his method of auditioning—teaching *all* of the auditioners a five-minute routine and song in one large group, (by rote if they can't read music). He feels you learn immediately who can sing and move, who is a quick study, etc. I may use this at my next tryouts.

There are many attributes I look for during auditions: stage presence, poise, body type, charisma, acting skill, projection, vocal variation, energy, appearance, a "certain sparkle," and an ability to respond to others and to me. There is also a special quality I look for, which is harder to define—one might call it a freshness or realness —an instinctive knowledge that makes that character come alive.

All too common is the director's dilemma of having to choose between two talents—for instance, one a singer who is a weak actor, the other an actor who has a small voice. If that happens to you, don't be afraid to tackle two evenings of callbacks if you think they're necessary. If people won't come back that often, you probably don't want them in your production. At our tryouts, some had chosen to audition for roles that were particularly unsuited to their own talents. When I asked them to read for other roles, I could see their dismay. They were simply not in touch with their own assets and limitations. I cast against type (see Glossary) and interracially when suitable.

Early Challenges

One faced early on was casting one of the leads. It was the typical choice, between a man with an excellent voice but who was only a fair actor and another who was an excellent actor, with an adequate voice. My first choice would have been the strong singer (because of this role and the demanding music), but it turned out that he was unable to begin rehearsals for ten days, and since the other man was able to start immediately, that solved the problem.

At the end of the evening, I asked for feedback from our production group.

My keen-eared musical director was sure of those she wanted to make up her singing ensemble. The choreographer needed more choices before making any final selections.

I still felt we had no one for the part of Marius (the young male lead), so we would have to cancel our first rehearsal in order to hold more auditions.

I suggested that we might take out casting ads in the newspapers and/or put a notice on one of the local radio stations. We decided on radio, as it gave a faster response and we were able to secure public service time, which was free. (If you do this, be aware that PSAs are broadcast during slow air time on commercial stations.)

I bring up this casting situation so that you will never cast a weaker person in a lead, even if you have to delay rehearsals. I missed three rehearsals in order to get the right talent, but this saved a great deal of time later, and the final result was stronger.

As luck (and breaks) would have it, by late the next evening we had found a potential Marius as well as two possible Panisses, an Admiral, and an Escartifique. They were asked to return for callbacks.

Three of the Fannys (no pun intended) would return to read. The singer called for Marius was to have been at the theatre by 9:00 p.m. At 10:00 p.m. he still hadn't shown, so we presumed he was not interested (since he didn't even call). I apologized and asked the women to come back. Yes, there would be more callbacks. If we had no Marius, we obviously could not go into rehearsal. Needless to say, I would never cast this man in any other show of mine.

Before our callbacks ended, one actress came to audition (at the last minute) for the part of Fanny. Charming, almost the right age, this new auditioner had an exquisite, classically trained, and expressive operatic soprano. My hopes were high as she was handed the script for a her reading. By way of relaxing her and explaining the play, I mentioned the charming movie of *Fanny*, starring Leslie Caron and Charles Boyer, and joked about how the lovely score was used only as background music and no one sang. When she opened her mouth to read, all hopes were dashed! She read with a flat, emotionless monotone; stumbling over words, smiling brightly as she spoke of Fanny's sadness. I would truly have loved to place this talented singer in the ensemble in order to try to help her acting, but I had been told she would definitely not accept a small role.

Some controversy had already developed when one long-time and well-respected theatre member was invited to callbacks for a part *he* felt was wrong for him. He had actually been studying another part for months and had even secured the aid of a vocal coach. So intent was he on having that role, that he insisted upon being given a second chance to audition. Unfortunately, neither his trim profile nor his acting style convinced anyone that he could play the other part.

Meanwhile, the casting continued with (now) two possible Fannys—one an attractive, dark-haired girl and the other a beautiful blonde. The dark-haired girl—the one I chose—had a lovely, naturalistic style, while the blonde was good but had a too-smooth gloss. Our only callback for Honorine (Fanny's mother) was a large but attractive woman with a powerhouse soprano. Yes, she might make an Honorine, but the casting of each other role was dependent on who played the leads.

True to the problems we had encountered throughout, one of the supporting roles offered was turned down. He preferred another—could he speak to the director personally? He could, of course. And did. We talked by phone for quite a while.

I returned to the production group, my hands tied in a manner of speaking. After consultation, amending my choice, I gave the singer in question the role he desired. I needed what he had to offer, age, style, etc., so through compromise (as there was no other possibility for his part in that age range), I'd won a war— the bigger picture—not a personal ego battle. It wasn't easy.

Since it was almost 10:30 p.m. and was getting too late to make more phone calls, we set up our final auditions for the next day.

By 8:00 p.m. the following evening, we began our *final, final* callbacks. Four actors were called forward to read for the parts of Brun, Escartifique, Cesar, and Panisse. Their energy, wit, and intelligent readings created one of the few magical moments of this otherwise exhausting time. Finally, by 10:30 p.m., we had made our choices (a Marius included) and by 11:00 had all our acceptances. Now for a peaceful night's sleep!

3

The Beginning: First Rehearsals

The ensemble and principals met for several rehearsals with the music director—I was unobtrusively present. She started with the group numbers and let cast members go home as they completed their responsibilities, leaving the principals to do their solos, duets, trios, etc. After several evenings of hard work, all had an understanding of the music and were asked to memorize the music *before* the first blocking rehearsal. Many had already.

Sample Rehearsal Schedule

Day 1	Production meeting		Day 4	Callbacks
Day 2	Tryouts		Day 5	Music
Day 3	Tryouts		Day 6	Music

TBA = To Be Announced. (Everyone please save these rehearsals, although you will not be needed at all of them.

Reh. 1 Read/sing-through, cast and crew.

Reh. 2 Music/Talking about characterization/Exercises
Dancers (*then on their own schedule*)
Production meeting (and each week afterward)

Reh. 3 Block Book, Act I

Reh. 4 Block Music, Act I

Reh. 5   Go over Music and Book I blocking (+ exercises)
Reh. 6   Block Book II, some Music II
Reh. 7   TBA*
            Production meeting
Reh. 8   Block rest of Music II and odds and ends
Reh. 9   Go over Act II blocking (+ exercises). Substitute props from now on.
Reh. 10 Go back to Act I, no scripts
Reh. 11 Go over Act I
Reh. 12 Dance and leads and ensemble blending
            Production meeting
Reh. 13 Act II, no scripts
Reh. 14 Go over Act II
Reh. 15 TBA
Reh. 16 Run I
Reh. 17 Run II
Reh. 18 Run II
Reh. 19 Music with orchestra
Reh. 20 TBA
Reh. 21 TBA and Dance
Reh. 22 Run
Reh. 23 Run onstage with Orchestra
            Production meeting
Reh. 24 Leads only and dancers, some singers (blending)
Reh. 25 TBA
Reh. 26 Run Act II twice, some costumes
Reh. 27 Run Act I twice, some costumes
Reh. 28 Dress rehearsal, no makeup
Reh. 29 Dress rehearsal, makeup optional
Reh. 30 Dress rehearsal (makeup parade first)
Reh. 31 Full dress rehearsal
            Preview
            Preview
            Opening night
(Sundays, there were sometimes afternoon and evening rehearsals.)

At the first read/sing-through with the entire company, I requested that the cast sit in a large circle, leaving a few empty chairs so the leads could move around and sit to talk or sing close to any character they were relating to. I asked the designers and crew heads to say a few words about themselves and what they were contributing so that we all would get to know one another. I started and then introduced our assistant director as someone the ensemble could go to anytime for help and guidance—I did not want them ever to feel that they were without someone for counseling if I seemed to be busy with the principals. I also asked each of the cast members to stand and tell us about themselves (one minute) and their characters (two minutes maximum).

I asked that in our first read/sing-through, that they please try to communicate with each other, rather than try to impress me. I assured them that they had already impressed me, or I would still be casting (by now, somewhat of an inside joke). What I wanted from them would be to connect with one another personally and emotionally.

Exercise

Before we started, I led a brief warm-up: asking all to stand (crew too), wiggle their toes, shake their wrists, move their elbow and shoulders. Then we did a series of dance/music warm-ups, led by our musical director and choreographer (no crew). Head rolls, arm rolls, legs and torsos stretching, lunges, and kicks readied their bodies. Diction and alphabet songs, performed in staccato and legato up and down the scales, readied their voices.

Our musical director suggested that in the future the cast sing in the car on the way to rehearsals. She asked them to hum softly at first and gradually increase the volume. She said that mouths that don't want to open wide and stiff jaws that don't want to move fast enough can be persuaded to do so.

As a further relaxer, I asked the cast to do an exercise in which they stand facing one another, paired in twos, look into each other's eyes (one minute), then close their eyes and explore one another's faces slowly with their hands—(both at the same time) so that they become familiar with the contours of each other's face (two minutes)—this was especially helpful to singers about to be family members and lovers. We then changed partners (several times). Marius (the son) and Cesar (his father) found this exercise particularly helpful for their budding relationship.

The stage manager also reintroduced the fact that the ensemble would be responsible for helping the crew with set changes so that the traffic backstage would be lessened. Each individual would be assigned a particular set part or piece of furniture to move, and this change would be choreographed early in rehearsal. The crew would be dressed in black or have costumes so as to fit into our production style.

I reiterated what I'd said to designers and crew heads, that everyone think of this as a play that just happens to have music and dance as part of it rather than a musical. There should be a family feeling to the show. I felt the audience would appreciate following the lives of identifiable characters on stage who continue to appear and reappear throughout the play, so they would be people rather than a "chorus."

Then, for more than two and a half hours, with only a short break, the cast read and sang. After all the preparation that had gone before, I felt, as did the designers and production crew, a measure of elation—although I felt the musical was too long. At long last we had a cast—a handsome group. I congratulated myself and co-workers for having done well. Mixed with that elation, however, was the certain knowledge that many hours of work would be needed to make this creation come alive, onstage.

My final words to the company that rehearsal were that the element missing in so many musicals, although there may be a great deal of energy onstage, is believable characters. Therefore, every cast member would write an autobiography of his or her character, trying to include the five most important events of the character's life. At the next rehearsal all cast members would exchange autobiographies.

"Please don't just 'think about it'—write your autobiographical thoughts down," I continued. There's something about the discipline of writing it down—the mind photographs, so you will remember it subliminally when you need to, even when you're onstage and under pressure, trying to remember your lines or singing. When you write the autobiography of your character, I prefer you to say 'I' rather than 'he' or 'she.' You need to know the character you're playing onstage as well as you know yourself. Since *verbs* are a key to doing, your autobiographies will be full of them." (Here are excerpts of two from our group.)

Sample Autobiographies (Abridged)

(Comments in parentheses are my notes to the cast member.)

Panisse
At the opening of the show I am 54, and in the family sailmaking business. Other family members own vineyards in other parts of France. As a boy I was fat and

Fanny, Act II, family reunion.

pudgy, and dominated by Cesar. I grinned and bore this in order to have friendships and attachments. I now pinch ladies' bottoms and show myself as a bon vivant as a cover-up for my own inadequacies and shyness. I live in the shadow of Cesar, who is macho. In the beginning I'm not in love with Fanny, but choose her to express my sexuality. I am aware that Fanny belongs in Cesar's family, and I try to "one-up" Cesar by taking Fanny as my wife. My character is somewhat more corpulent than I am. I relate to Cesar, Escartifique, and Brun because I am forced into their company and there is no one else. (*The male bravado and camaraderie they all showed was simply how men were raised to behave; yet it was also a bond that held the men together.*) My relations with Cesar change in Act II, as does my status. There is a strong bond with Cesar as we love Cesario, the son. (*Panisse and Cesar are both wrapped up in Fanny; Cesar is Fanny's "surrogate" father.*) I worship the ground Cesario walks on, and am very indulgent of him. In Act II, I'm dying of arteriosclerosis, from eating and and drinking too much, and in love with Fanny. (*Please go back and find the five most important events in his life.*)

Cesar
I am more ruled by my heart than by good sense, as opposed to Panisse. I expect the sun to shine, or I'll have to speak to the clouds. I am generous to a fault with the ladies, and I like women of all sizes and shapes. Marius's mother, my wife,

died in childbirth. (*It could be his wife was his true love.*) I am a cafe owner and am the center of things; everyone comes to me. I am good-humored and do what Marius rejects by running this tavern owned by our family for generations. Although I'm on my son Marius's case, I would walk over hot coals for him. I don't mean half the stuff I say to Marius. I'm not a verbal type person with those close to me and don't know how to say "I care" to Marius. (*Remember that many Europeans use their hands more, and are, in general, more outwardly emotional than Americans.*) I soften in Act II and dote on Cesario. I learn not to be the boss so much. I mellow from a grizzly to a teddy-bear. (*Director again! If you can get the bull-in-the-china-shop character in Act I, a softer man in Act II will be a nice contrast.*)

Blocking

Blocking, as you know, is the process of determining where and how the cast move about the stage as they say their lines and sing.

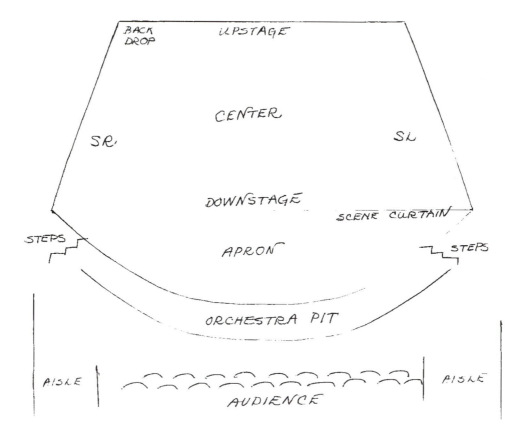

The clean wood floor of the rehearsal room was now spiked (marked) with masking tape defining the floorplan of the sets. Red tape marked the walls, doors, exits, and entrance ways for Act I. Green tape defined the set of Act II. Plain white tape represented the fixed portions that would remain throughout both acts.

The assistant director reminds how important it is for the cast to put in their scripts (in their own understandable shorthand), where they are blocked. Such blocking shorthand notations as those described here are commonly used shortcuts:

(sit) ↓   (rise) ↑   (cross left) = XL

(cross upright center) =   XURC

I had blocked the entire musical previously, and all was marked in my director's book. In the libretto sections (leads only) I requested that they first move about saying their lines according to what felt most comfortable for them. There would be no "right" or "wrong" at this juncture—this blocking was not cast in concrete, just an experiment. We would zero in on final moves later. (Obviously, this is *not* possible with an inexperienced cast or for musical numbers or ensemble sections.)

As we worked, the stage manager entered everything in his Production Book. I had already worked out my staging, and the stage manager put the cast's movements in pencil in his book. That way, many times there were two choices for blocking: I could suggest that each do what I had previously thought out or use what the leads had come up with. These suggestions were often exciting (usually the most interesting blocking is a combination).

There is no magic to staging a musical number, it is the same as blocking a scene. You find out what the needs of that song are and what the emotional wants are. Then listen to the music over and over and, as I said in the previous chapter, it will tell *you* when to tell the cast to kick, to stand, when to use their hands, arms, when to hug, where the ensemble should move, if the lead should move away from the ensemble to center stage, etc. As director, ask yourself, WHAT DOES THE MUSIC TELL YOUR BODY THE CHARACTER SHOULD DO, then do it, write it in your script, and pass it along to the cast.

Try to fill every inch of the stage—and not have everyone on the same level. (Have some standing, sitting, on steps, on platforms.) Help the cast make it look easy, true, recreating what the character might do in life.

Focus is what the audience looks at. Sometimes what you want is the soloists downstage and the chorus upstage or change the focus with the chorus temporarily downstage, mixing with the principals (so there can be interaction). Arrange actor/singers on stage so that the audience looks at the person(s) you

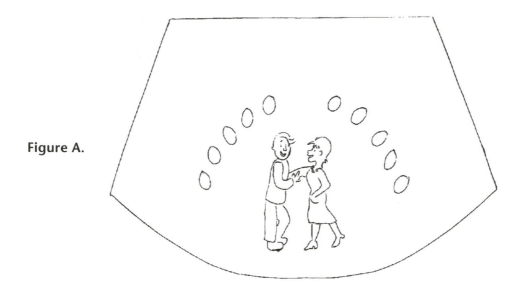

Figure A.

want them to at any given moment. For instance, you can seat your chorus, your leads can be standing, or vice versa (see figure A). You can separate the actor—the lead—from the crowd, making him or her the apex of a triangle (see figure B). Also, use semicircle or straight lines for smaller groups. (For theatre in the round or central arena staging—see Alexander Dean and Lawrence Carra, *Fundamentals of Play Directing*, Holt, Rinehart and Winston, p. 290.)

Figure B.

Staging The Musical Numbers

Here are some of the ideas and staging I used in *Fanny*. The diagrams that follow will make it easy for you to visualize these numbers rather than just read about them.

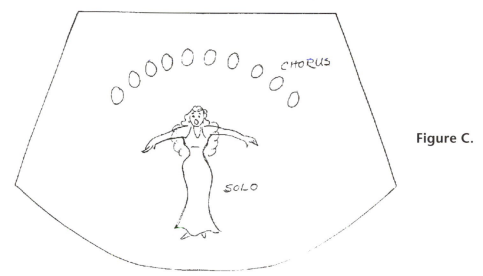

Figure C.

In one number because the singer's voice wasn't strong, she needed to be near the chorus, so I placed them in a semicircle behind her, with some sitting, some on their knees, and others standing or leaning. In that way she had the vocal support of the ensemble, but the focus of the number was still hers (see figure C).

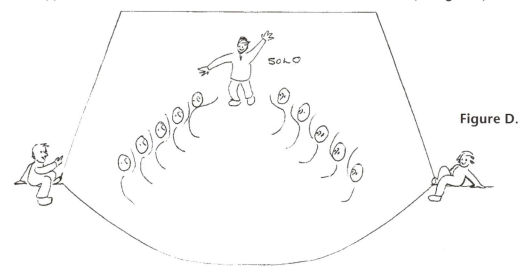

Figure D.

It was a question of sitting in the rehearsal room and joking, "Please do not put your hand in front of Fanny while she is singing her solo." "Ensemble, do not move or scratch when Marius is proposing to her," etc.

In the number "Restless Heart," in which there was a strong singer and the all-male ensemble, I asked the ensemble to come downstage, use all parts of the set, hang from ladders and lounge on fishbaskets, blocking the actors/singers to lift Marius up and carry him around. I felt that could work because the men in the ensemble were physically strong, and Marius could sing upside down on a trapeze if asked (see figure D on page 39).

Figure E.

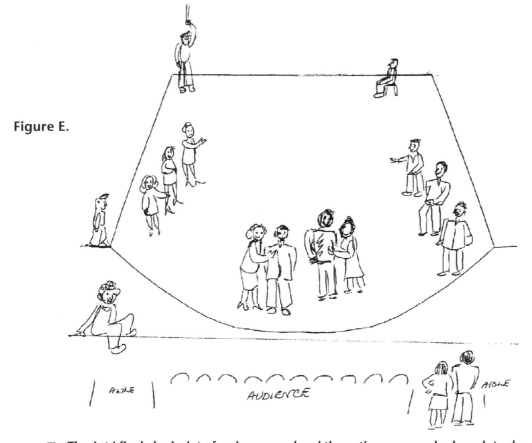

The Act I finale had a lot of racing around and the entire company had much to do, running in and out of the house and trying to get together (eventually) to make a strong Act I curtain. So we placed the principals in pairs at center, and had them change sides from time to time. The ensemble was lined up all along the sides of the stage and out into the front of the auditorium. Further focus was later provided by the light designer with specials for the four leads (see figure E on page 40).

This worked very well, as it gave variety, and was not difficult to learn, especially with the expert staging of our choreographer.

For contrast, at the beginning of Act II, there was a charming, quiet number, and as I originally planned, I sat everyone on the edge of the stage and let the follow spot fall on each individually as they had something special to sing. It was attention getting and a romantic opening for the first moments after the intermission. We tried the reprise, in which we had a mature Marius and Fanny with their 16-year-old son. So I asked the trio to think of what they might be doing if this were real life, and the young man playing the son said, "I would want to play a game with my father." So they played a simple game of basketball. After the two males played, I asked that they include Fanny in the game, and it worked theatrically, *humanly*, and psychologically for the song, because it was father and son, then mother, father, and son. Much stronger than my original concept!

Other ideas: you might want to move the ensemble in counterpoint to the lead, or put them behind the lead, just swaying. Vary your staging to support the leads. Put your chorus stage left one time, stage right another; and upstage yet another; your leads on steps or stools for focus or have them moving in and out and around and through the ensemble.

If a song is particularly difficult to project, and you've cast someone who is more of an actor than a singer, add the chorus into part of the song and move the soloist downstage. (Of course, if you have someone as strong as Kevin Kline or Mandy Patinkin singing, you don't want or need anyone "helping.") Again, I mark all of this in my score, which is in my Director's Book, before working with the cast. My markings say, "Move two steps to the left here, four steps forward and hands up and sway to the right here." If I need some help with difficult steps, I'll ask the choreographer, who can translate what I'm thinking into making the performers' feet, hands, and body move. After listening to the music yet again, it said, "move them here, or they should stand still here." I asked myself, will the performers be able to do the staging that I've done, and if not, I'll change to something they *can* do. (The important thing when you're staging any production, is to help the cast to bring their own sense to the blocking, helping you to shape the action.) Thinking of the time frame in which the songs in *Fanny* take place (early 1900s) and that most of the women would have long skirts—and the men should be more like fishermen than a chorus—we tried to bring all of this into the movements and staging.

Remember, you can move a solo or duo number downstage, in front of the main set; close or drop the scene curtain (giving an opportunity to change the set behind the curtain) so as to minimize the next scene change time.

Each song of a musical is like a scene of a play. If you think of it that way, what seems like a huge task is easier. When in doubt, remember that less is more. You do not need to have everyone moving constantly; it blurs the lyric and is more difficult for performers to sing when moving *too* much. The sound of many people singing on a stage is interesting in itself, and an entire group uniformly executing arm movements can be simple and charming. See Appendix III by Nancy Vunovich PhD. She has additional tips on staging.

Each musical has several types of numbers that are similar to numbers in other musicals. Without too much generalizing, the ensemble numbers, solos, and duets in *Chess* and *Carnival* have a certain similarity to the numbers in *The Sound of Music* and *Miss Saigon.* I don't mean in the feelings of the songs, but in how they might be generally staged. Let's look at the overall picture. There's usually a boy-meets-girl number, a company number with two or three of the leads, a large chorus number with everyone. Here is a comparison chart of similarities in musical numbers.

Comparison of Similarities in Musical Numbers

Musical	Solo	Duo/Trio	Chorus
Fiddler on the Roof	Now I Have Everything	Matchmaker	Sunrise, Sunset
Music Man	My White Knight	Pick a Little, Talk a Little	76 Trombones
Hello, Dolly	Ribbons Down My Back	It Takes a Woman	Put on Your Sunday Clothes
Man of La Mancha	The Impossible Dream	Dulcinea	Knights of the Willful Countenance
Anything Goes	Easy to Love	You're the Top	Anything Goes
The Sound of Music	The Sound of Music	Maria	Do Re Mi
Grand Hotel	Bonjour Amour	Who Couldn't Dance With You	We'll Take a Glass Together

As you do more musicals, your job becomes a great deal easier because blocking (or staging) *ideas* that work in one musical number can quite often work, with proper adaptation, to the needs of the current production. *This does not in any way diminish your creative contribution.* It is, of course, general and overly simplistic in one sense, but is true nonetheless.

Putting Together a Multicultural Musical Revue

As this book proceeds, I am planning and working on a musical revue based on Harlem Renaissance music, to be performed at Mt. Vernon College in Washington, D.C. I had originally though that this section would be in the appendix, but in further trying to explain the creative process (an impossible task and so different in each of us), I realized that the specifics here are pertinent to the thinking that goes on while directing a musical. The joy of working with and casting senior citizens and minorities cannot be over-rated. This will not only expand our (your) production but the audience's experience as well.

When word got around about open casting, many fine singer/actors (most of whom I did not know) turned up at tryouts. The casting of the four roles was fun and I always enjoy the challenge of working with new talent.

There are to be twenty numbers in the production. I've been trying to decide what the center of each number is, what part of the set each one should be staged on, what the lighting and costuming might be, and how to fit each song into the theme of the evening. What I've done is listen to the music and attempt to see what each song says to me. For instance, in one by W. C. Handy I keep having an image of a charming, elegant woman pulling

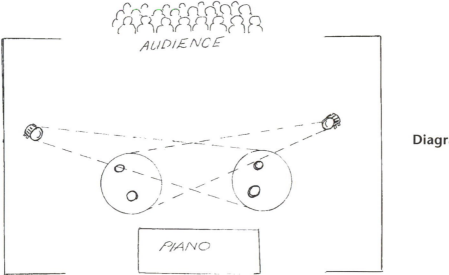

Diagram A.

a feather boa. In the staging I have been using that image and the whole number seems to be falling into place easily and quickly. The costume is to be pink so I though we would have a bright spot light and a huge feather boa. The lighting designer wants to use four specials across the stage—and not a spot—for a more dramatic effect (see Diagram A on page 43). The number will follow this pattern (Diagram B):

Diagram B.

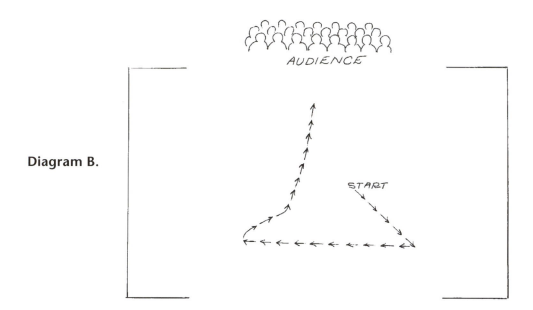

Listening to the song, "Black and Blue," to be performed by the four singer/actors, it seemed that they might begin far away from each other (each at a corner of the stage), but as the music builds come together center and make a circle almost like a marching band in a dream-like state (see Diagram C on page 45).

The number then has a dirge quality, which adds to the seriousness and beauty of it. We will do it centerstage because of its place in the revue between two solo numbers, one on stage left and the other stage right. Lighting will be mostly blue and then hot, maybe red (we think right now), perhaps with just a spot center at the very end.

These are examples of how I work out a song's possible staging. Of course, the actual movements within the framework of the song—that is, when the

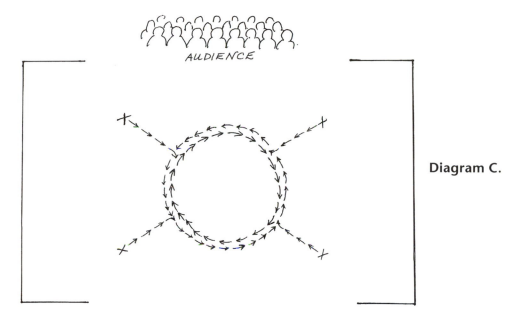

Diagram C.

performers should move to down left or up right, fast or slow, etc.—come from what the lyrics say.

Here is what the stage will look like (Diagram D).

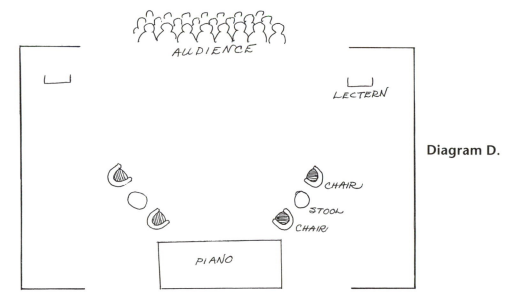

Diagram D.

The cast of the
multi-cultural
Revue; Mount
Vernon College,
Washington,
D.C.

Here is a list of the musical numbers and my staging ideas:

Musical Number	Staging Ideas	Cast
Eubie Blake "The Slow Drag"	Use mirror ball.	Piano solo
George Gershwin from *Porgy and Bess* "There's a Boat Leaving Soon . . ."	By piano USC.	Male solo
Irving Berlin from *As Thousands Cheer* "Harlem on My Mind" "What'll I Do?"	Blue spot, stool SL. cigarette; leaning proscenium SR.	Female solo Male solo
Thomas "Fats" Waller "This Joint Is Jumpin'" "Black and Blue"	Brights lights all over. See description page 44.	Female solo Quartet

Musical Number	Staging Ideas	Cast
Eubie Blake/ Andy Razaf from *Blackbirds,* "You're Lucky to Me"	Move chair CS straddle it.	Male solo
Thomas "Fats" Waller "Honeysuckle Rose"	2 stools; women sing back to back involving men in second verse.	Female duet
Arthur Herzog, Jr./ Billie Holiday "God Bless the Child"	Kneeling center, spot; bring a child from audience to sing to (plant).	Male solo
Eubie Blake/Nobel Sissle from *Shuffle Along* "If You've Never Been Vamped by a Brownskin"	Fringed dress; shake and move all over stage area.	Female solo
Margaret Bonds/ Langston Hughes (art/spiritual) "The Negro Speaks of Rivers"	Spot in section of balcony where all can see her.	Female solo
George Gershwin "Clap Yo' Hands"	Choreographer will stage	M/F duet
Scott Joplin from *Treemonisha* "Wrong Is Never Right"	Piano DSC; he leans on it, gives advice— casual, elegant.	Male solo
Duke Ellington "It Don't Mean a Thing If It Ain't Got Swing"	C. hot lites that jump to blue to "doowahs"	Male solo

Musical Number	Staging Ideas	Cast
Thomas "Fats" Waller "Squeeze Me"	She, on his lap— sugar daddy; he removes her jewelry during song; a refined strip.	M/F duet
George Gershwin "The Man I Love"	Sitting on piano in spot.	Female solo
James P. Johnson from *Runnin' Wild* "Charleston"	To be staged by choreographer	Trio
Duke Ellington "Mood Indigo"	In audience, singing to lady on the aisle.	Male solo
W. C. Handy "St. Louis (Woman) Blues"	White boa (as described previously).	Female solo
George Gershwin from *Porgy and Bess* "It Ain't Necessarily So"	To be staged by choreographer; end with mirror ball before curtain call.	Quartet

Because of an unexpected and sudden change in my business travel at the Kennedy Center, I had to ask the producer to turn the direction over to another person; and I never got to see the finished production. These notes remain valid for my concept and I hope to do this Revue next season.

4

Working with Singer/Dancers on Acting: The Early Stages

> Directing is problem solving. Your work, your art, is your life; enter into it with an open heart and an open mind. Be sure when you're directing that you do not presume to know all of the answers on the first day of rehearsal. Miracles are possible—just be cautious.
>
> —*Gerald Freedman,*
> *in a workshop at the Kennedy Center*
> *American College Theatre Festival.*

As directors we sometimes get in the way of allowing the cast to do their best work. Be super sensitive, have your radar in place to observe and try to sense what is going on in their psyches. Be ever cautious not to jump the gun, or to say "*no*" too soon. The company needs time to express themselves and time for things to take root; help them to do that. YET IT IS MOST IMPORTANT TO BE SPECIFIC AND *GIVE CONSTANT FEEDBACK* ABOUT HOW AND WHAT THEY ARE DOING OR *NOT* DOING.

With that in mind, I also *try* never to lose my temper (somewhat of a miracle). I'm always sorry when I do, because it tightens people and they can't give their best. Create a relaxed atmosphere for the cast to work in, even if it's painful to your own ego.

Take time during the second week of rehearsals to explore (briefly) the art and craft of acting, especially to greener members of the group. My experience is that acting is the weakest part of many musical productions.

To counteract this—try the following:

> In order to play a scene truthfully, an actor must reduce the script to its basic units [or beats]. For every beat there must be a different objective for the character. Objective is another word for *need*. Keeping the objective in mind at all times is the key to acting. In most cases it is not what is found *in* the text, but what is *underneath* the text, what some call the "subtext," which is important. You react just as you would react as a person, to stimuli. Only sometimes the stimuli are imaginary. In rehearsals we get physical tension and emotional tension out of the way so we can use our own senses. (Lee Strasberg Theatre Institute, Anna Strasberg, director.)

PLEASE NOTE THAT *BEATS* AND *SUBTEXT* ARE JUST AS APPLICABLE WHEN WORKING ON *LYRICS* AS WITH THE BOOK SECTIONS!

For instance, a strong beat (unit) for Fanny is, "I want to convince Marius I love him so he returns my love."

So, for our next rehearsal I asked each cast member to break his/her part (including the lyrics) down into beats (emotional changes, or turning points) and mark them in pencil in their scripts. That is, take each page of the script and mark where the character's emotions change. In this way each would know that in this part of the dialogue *or lyric* there are X number of emotional changes. Then, next to the beat changes, I asked that each performer note what the character is experiencing internally (subtext), versus what he/she is actually saying or singing. On each page we'll have all the emotional changes the character is experiencing and the processes—and feelings—beneath those emotions.

If an emotion is pleasurable, it makes the character happy, and it *affects the body*. The body smiles, the eyes sparkle. The opposite is true as well. If the character is angry, the eyes might squint and the body tense up. If the character is reacting to someone and finds him or her dull, the eyes droop or close and one might want to nap. *Acting is mind, heart (emotions), and body—and, of course, imagination.*

Anyone can learn to use the four faculties—mind, emotions, body, and imagination—to his or her advantage. The goal is to help your company to use all four. Some might scream: "I despise you, I despise you!" and their bodies would be limp. You know then that their emotions went from their mind and somehow skipped the heart and the guts—their own body language gives them away.

One of the simplest yet all-encompassing definitions of acting is: "Acting is living truthfully in imaginary circumstances." This is attributed to master teacher Sanford Meisner of New York's Neighborhood Playhouse. In working toward this living truthfully (using their imaginations), singers take images into their brain, then the images flow through it to their heart, this causes an emotional reaction that fills their *entire* bodies as they *react* emotionally. To act is to *be*—to really *listen*, to let stimuli go deep down into the heart and soul and help the *body react* totally. If a cast member reacts to any situation, it will show in the arms, knees, face—everywhere. Acting is not just a matter of giving proper line readings, but of responding with one's entire being. An actor/singer who is weeping will certainly not convince an audience he is truly anguished if his body is only half involved. The emotional reaction must show clear down to the feet and up and out through the fingertips (in songs as well).

Exercise

Body language can really give singers away. If they're singing, "Oh, boy am I happy!," but it is just coming from the face and not their whole beings, then finding, visualizing, and acting out an animal characterization can help singer/dancers find the physicalization and body freedom to become someone else. As an *example*, here is a story on animal characterization with a cast rehearsing a proposed musical version of *A Streetcar Named Desire*. The director said, "I want you to think and then find an animal your character suggests, then communicate with each other as that animal, using sounds and body movements." (No dialogue.) The singer playing Stanley chose an ape and the actress playing Blanche chose a butterfly, and all the way through the exercise there was a tug of war between the two, using sounds, body, and heart. They then returned to Tennessee Williams's words and the new music and were able to express the emotions vividly, finding new walks and ways to execute the smallest actions.

Start with, "Think of an animal your character reminds you of, and, with one or two partners, get up and move and interact as that animal, with sounds but *no* words (two–four minutes). Be sure to get the animal into your body with energy. Then go back to the words and the lyrics and music and see what has been discovered." (This can work wonders with the *emotions* behind the lyrics for singers who have little acting experience, and free their bodies in the bargain.)

This is not a mental exercise but an on-your-feet physical and emotional experience.

One cast member said, "I'm having trouble visualizing what my character looks like," so I asked him to chart the character throughout an average day, from the time the alarm goes off in the morning (or however he gets up) until the time the character goes to sleep, including eating meals, going to work, or doing whatever there is to do around the house. Write all this down. Then *walk through* the high points of the character's daily routine. This helped with his character's walk and interaction with the rest of the cast.

Exploring the character's value system can also help if the scene involves love—how do the characters value sex or making love, and how do they go about finding it in their lives; what, if any, is their sense of humor like? These strong life forces need to be explored (some only verbally).

After using these techniques for a rehearsal or two, some of the *Fanny* company appeared elated. These techniques are hardly new; they come from Stanislavski's and Vakhtangov's* (see Glossary) invaluable writing, expounded upon later by such artists as Uta Hagen and Viola Spolin (see bibliography).

I always ask for an extra week of rehearsal so as to use these exercises. (See Rehearsal Schedule, pages 31 and 32.) In the schedule I have "trouble spots" or TBA (To Be Announced) listed once a week with the entire company. At those times I can use these theatre games and growth exercises as needed.

At the next rehearsal we worked on what I hoped would become a highly charged and romantic love scene, where Marius picks Fanny up in his arms and carries her to his bedroom. But in this phase of the blocking, when unfamiliarity and actors' nervousness still prevailed, it was translated into "scoop, kiss, and skedaddle!" Everyone smiled as the two romantic leads, scripts flying, made their first awkward attempt at creating this passionate moment.

Later, Fanny was preparing for her love song with Marius. The tension mounted, the musical introduction of the song built to a climax, Fanny took a breath—and Marius promptly forgot his line to cue Fanny's song. So we stopped and I used the animal exercise just mentioned.

Flexibility and an ability to incorporate changes are essential. Also, judging from this rehearsal, a good sense of humor is *highly* recommended and *necessary*.

Many old musicals like *Fanny* are a little dated and the exposition is fuzzy. For instance, Marius, the young male lead, after being the center of Act I, has little to do in the first half of Act II. So, in order to compensate for this, I placed him onstage (USR) in Act II to read along with Fanny (DSC) his letter to her from overseas, bringing him back to the center of the action rather than leaving him offstage. This double focus was quite romantic as well.

As the evening progressed, I encouraged the cast to stay open, try new things, keep experimenting. In this way, their characters would become bigger, fuller, richer, more complete. And that advice went for this director as well. "Keep open, keep expanding."

Where Are We?

By this time (end of week II) our musical was mostly staged. The cast had been given ample opportunity to exchange biographies and tell each other about their characters and were busy learning the choreography.

An actor's responsibility to the rest of the cast is great. Theatre is not an individual art, like painting, but a creative effort involving the talents and contributions of many people. The interdependency of each theatrical artist upon the other is what makes theatre the unique, exciting, and sometimes frustrating experience it can be.

With this in mind, I felt it necessary to speak to some in the cast about coming late to rehearsals and how that undermined the entire production.

As per the rehearsal schedule, I asked that scripts be down (lines and songs memorized) for Act I.

The first day the cast put down their scripts I tried to be very quiet. It was a difficult time because yesterday, with scripts in hand, they were progressing, and suddenly, without scripts, the magic was gone. Some didn't know where they were or what the devil their lines were. Sensing this could happen, I had broken the act down into four- or five-page segments; we did those four or five pages, and then I said, "*Stop*, go back." They did, and then went on to do the next four or five pages (and so on); this helped all to memorize the words *with* the blocking. It always is a slow stage in rehearsals, but one we had to live through, and it continued an important step in the cast/director trust and growth ritual.

A BIG hurdle remained. The cast would have to truly commit to *relating* to one another. At this point few in the company were responding enough to the others. Although, individually, most of the leads were doing their own thing reasonably well, they seemed much of the time unable to connect to other cast members' characterizations. This is not unusual, but a normal part of the rehearsal process. There are, indeed, so many things to concentrate on—lines, blocking, music, voice, emotion, characterization—that it is understandable. Yet, once the show opens, it can make for a dreary evening for the audience, watching a performance by a cast whose members are not relating, but only doing "their own part." For instance, if Marius causes Fanny to react, that makes an action and then a reaction—and the feelings snowball to the rest of the group, as it does in our everyday lives. These reactions and feelings are recognized and absorbed by the cast. The emotional result pleases and focuses the audience during the performance.

After doing their lines "off book" for several days, both remarkable and horrendous things began to happen. Cast members looked into each other's eyes, made connections, responded, yet sometimes also totally forgot simple blocking moves they had made before without difficulty. Yet magical moments occurred as each one's response to the other triggered the emotions of all.

I reminded the entire cast that they really must continue observing one another. To make my point, I joked that if the actress playing Fanny walked in without her blouse, it would be an hour before anyone would notice. They laughed in acknowledgment of being in their own worlds, of concentrating so hard on their characters that they were hardly aware of the others. Truly, there were a lot of unnecessary pauses in tonight's rehearsal. The leads sang over each other's lyrics, and one actually referred to her character's autobiography as her "obituary."

I knew that they were still fighting for the words and emotions to combine. Meanwhile, I tried to give encouragement and reinforcement where I could, saying, "Yes, that's coming along," or "Let's try this again, *another* way," etc.

Listening: A Most Important Tool

One of the keys to acting and characterization is to *listen* to what the other cast members say and sing, and then to react emotionally, physically. A weakness with many in the cast was that they only knew their own lines and didn't really listen to their colleagues, so they didn't feel and therefore couldn't react. True listening will make bodies react. (See exercise in chapter 7, "Preview," page 89.)

> A problem for the cast to solve was that in everyday life, people don't always LOOK at the person they're talking to. When I found the cast staring at each other continually (yet not listening), I gave them such tasks as setting the table, cleaning fish, hanging laundry, etc., which forced them to listen or they would miss their cue.
>
> "Listen—listen to the others! Please react and then sing," I said. This is particularly important so that there is a give and take *during* a song. It involves trusting. The intimacy and sense of camaraderie that develops is an adventure very special to theatre.

Here is some fascinating advice from Tony Barr, former vice president of CBS, from his book *Acting for the Camera*. "Listen with your five senses, not just the ears.

> If I had to answer the question, "What is the most important ability for an actor?" there would be no contest. The answer would emphatically be *listening*.
>
> Lest there be some misunderstanding, let me define what I mean by listening. I am talking about *listening with all the senses*. In other words, listening involves more than what you hear: it involves what you see; it involves the responses of all of your senses; and, very importantly, it involves what you perceive intuitively and emotionally and what you have experienced and perceived in the past."

Exercise (by Tony Barr)

We do a simple listening exercise in the classroom. I learned it during a series of special sessions conducted by an extraordinary psychologist, Dr. Nathaniel Branden. Branden conducted seven sessions with a select group of our students, exploring some of the techniques he uses in psychotherapy to see if we could find some that would benefit actors without their becoming involved in therapy. Out of these remarkable sessions this exercise stood out above all the rest.

Two of the cast sit on the floor facing each other, as close as they can be without touching, and get into any position that is comfortable for them. One is the listener; the other is the speaker. The listener has absolutely no obligation in this exercise, except to look directly at the other person and to listen fully. He need not make responses of any nature whatsoever, but if he feels he wants to, or if he makes an involuntary one, that is fine. If nothing happens, that's also fine. In other words, the listener should have no need or wish to perform, just simply to listen.

The listener learns that if he trusts to listening, he will perceive things that he would not otherwise perceive. Most importantly, he will begin to feel. Frequently, the process of listening in itself will generate emotion, and the actor's biggest problem in most cases is to generate genuine emotion in imaginary circumstances.

Let's not kid ourselves; we are terrified that we will forget the line, and the whole process of remembering and saying the words not only takes our minds off what's happening in the scene, but also makes it impossible for us to listen to everything that's going on.

Characterization

Characterization can be defined as the creation of the ongoing reproduction of people; the traits that form an individual's nature.

TRY NOT TO IMPOSE CHARACTERIZATION!

All in all, building a character is much like using clay to build a piece of sculpture. Like choreographing a musical number, the sculptor adds a little

Scene from *Foxfire,* directed by David Young at the University of Missouri, Columbia, Summer Repertory Theatre.

clay here, chips away a little there. The same is true for our company members. Eventually this "clay" figure of Fanny would jump inside Fanny, and she would be both herself and her vision (the sculpture) of Fanny. That's why Stanislavski called it *building a character.* See Constantin Stanislavski's, *Building A Character,* New York: Routledge, Chapman, and Hall, 1988.

Characterization grows out of connections among the cast (listening) and evolves out of the action of the song or the libretto. It is released from *inside*! It is a process that brings to light what is buried at the very center (heart) of each character. Once this core (or SPINE) of the character is found, it's only a matter of helping to mold it like a piece of sculpture. By "spine" I mean the physical backbone and emotional makeup of the character.

> **Sample: I asked at the next *Fanny* rehearsal, "What's the spine of your character psychologically? What's the spine of the character physically?"**
>
> **The company had 15 minutes to prepare, and then each was asked to express and demonstrate for 60 to 90 seconds first their physical and then their psychological (emotional) spines. Again, *no words.* Just body and feelings (sounds are okay).**

Exercise

Characterization also grows out of the characters' connections to their environment. If your cast isn't using the environment, suggest a situation that requires them to pay attention to it. Ask them to SHOW (not tell) where they are, then BE in that environment—first alone (no words), then with another cast member—in their own words. Take two minutes for each time. Then for *fun* ask them to sing the same exercises in which they make up the tune and the words. It's a relaxer and adds *lots* of laughter and growth.

In another exercise, I suggested to the old Admiral and young Marius that they envision themselves on a quiet, foggy beach. The Admiral and about-to-be Sailor were to communicate and try to find out something very personal about one other, while being highly aware physically of their surroundings—wind, water, sand, sky.

One of the cast said to me privately, "Sometimes I feel we can't afford the time to do these exercises." My response was, "You can't afford *not to*—because if you don't, your character won't have the proper foundation—building a character is like building a house! No solid foundation, no full, rounded characterization."

Think Time for the Director

I tried to allow myself "THINK time" after every other rehearsal. "What am I trying to do, now? Next? Am I on schedule?"

Here are some specifics. "Marius, the young male lead, should have been more fun (he's stiff, so the audience will not take him to their hearts as they should). Unlike the actor playing Cesar, his father, who had a lot of personal, Gallic-like energy and humor, Marius is too macho American and tight. Also, the rhythm of the actor playing Panisse is too slow for his character's age in Act I (and this tended to slow up the rest of the company). Fanny, the leading lady, was not truly innocent—she was still *pretending* to be. Honorine, the fishmonger and Fanny's mother, was not really coarse enough and was holding onto playing nice." I tried to adjust all of this in the next rehearsals by exploring the problems, specifically, and by using improvisation to expand the characters' emotional development. Results are reported in the next chapter.

Some of my own handiwork now seemed fussy, so I asked Marius and Cesar to play their father-son talk quietly, more intimately, even if I had blocked them on opposite sides of a long table. (Obviously, I would have to change the blocking.)

Later, when Cesar was supposed to dance with Fanny, the simple choreography proved so perplexing that he jokingly asked for a stuntman.

During the scene when Cesar returns from his rendezvous, I suggested that he did not look like a man who had just enjoyed a lady's favors. We decided that he would enter smiling, with his walking-stick dragging behind him. This symbolism would be enjoyable and familiar to some in our audience. So! We were *progressing*.

Remember, any success you have in freeing people or in solving their problems will be duly noticed by the other cast members; seeing what you've done with one talent will inspire confidence. DISCOVERY IS CONTAGIOUS!

Improvisation Theatre Games— To Help Strengthen and *Enliven* Rehearsals as the Pressure Begins

Improvisation: "The act of playing, reciting, or singing extemporaneously."

Improvising is putting actor/singer/dancers in situations similar to the one in their scene or song, but changing the milieu and having them use their *own words*. The theory is that they will say and do, with their own words and actions, something similar to what is going on in the libretto or lyric, and through this, come to understand and expand their characters' goals more fully (and find the freedom to listen with their entire being). The improv should be tied in emotionally to the subject of the song or scene.

Sceptics who claim improvs are only a classroom tool probably don't experiment enough. Asking this cast to use their own words and emotions helped them to uncover their characters' basic needs. It freed them from the confines of the author and from memorization. Improvs helped them to understand *why* they were singing the words, and allowed them to feel the emotions *behind* the words, to draw upon their imagination to expand more of the inner part of their characterization.

> As I have mentioned, I realized that we had gone over and over things in rehearsal, but the result still wasn't deep *enough*; therefore, we had to get underneath defenses.

Exercise

The assistant director and I thought out several parallel situations, in which people had basically the same problems as Fanny, Marius, and their parents and asked each of the leads to share his or her character's innermost feelings in this situation but in their *own* words, asking that they be truly honest in this safe environment (closed rehearsal). Instinctively, they built a feeling similar to the emotions in our musical, because it was already in their psyche. Emotions surfaced more directly in the improv—most of the cast were overjoyed to have something new to share with the others. Immediately after each improv, I asked that they do the scene or song as written and use all of that feeling from the improv.

Several moments were lovely, personal—not forced or "actorish." I shared, "When you worked this time, you didn't pretend, you *were* the character." Improvs worked beautifully to heighten the honesty (and simplicity) of our two love songs. Your romantic leads are probably not going to fall in love during the first rehearsals (although ours did by opening night), so use these exercises to help them— obviously, not to fall in love but to look and feel like they have.

This entire process took only about two-and-a-half hours (working only with the principals). Note: We should have done this with the ensemble as well, as we learned when some of the reviews appeared. Improvisation helped to strengthen what held the people in our production together. I used the time that was built into the rehearsal schedule marked TBA for improvs and exercises. Reminder: sometimes these results can take a day to surface.

I was especially pleased with Fanny, whose voice was getting stronger as her characterization took over. All the improvs and exercises were giving her freedom, and other cast members were noticing. As with many improv exercises, after the cast experience freedom once or twice, they become relaxed about using others. I was gratified . . . for the moment.

5

Specific Challenges—Midway

Pulling the Musical Numbers Together

We took the entire next rehearsals to go over *each* musical number twice. We did the number, then I gave notes; repeated the number, then new notes.

I wanted to be sure our cast understood what the musical's progression was so they could be sure their *characterizations* fit. Then I asked a lot of questions, for instance, "What is going on in your mind when you sing that, how does your character really feel, happy, sad—what? Why doesn't that affect how you sing? Let *me* see and feel it, please! And *listen*—remember it's a key to reacting while singing." This exercise was very helpful at this point, for exploring new ideas and not repeating the same thing at every rehearsal.

Exercise

Let the music support you; close your eyes, relax into the music; experience it like you are hearing it for the first time; enjoy; move freely; do anything you want to. Hum as you're moving; then add the lyrics; then add blocking. We discovered some excellent body freedom for the solos, and I changed some stiff blocking to the more relaxed movement we found.

Talking about Comedy

In her fine book, *The Craft of Comedy* (Theatre Arts Books, 1957), Athene Seyler reminds us of the *art* of, and in, comedy, and gives us a practical down-to-earth guide. In *Fanny* it was most useful for the second leads, Brun and Escartifique (who are in the script primarily for comic relief), to use and apply the exercise in her book. Here is a quote from Ms. Seyler that was helpful:

> Now then, what is the root of comedy? The essentials are lack of balance, distortion, overemphasis, underemphasis, and surprise. All of these things are relative to what is the truth. First see the truth of the character, before you upset the balance. But you believe in the distorted part of the truth you've discovered.

BUT:

> . . . distorting that truth is what gets you the laugh, and believing in that distortion is what I find so interesting because when you play true character and get legit laughs from character, it's like you are slipping on a banana peel. In essence you are, in comedy, and that's what gives us the surprise and allows us to laugh.

She continues:

> Pay particular attention to key word or last word in a *cue* line; if it is not heard, there will be no laugh! So ENUNCIATE.

We constantly used this wonderful and little-known book during our rehearsals. The cast read their favorite sections to one another on break.

Farce—A Special Kind of Comedy

For a card game scene (which was in our musical to pick up and lighten the pace), we experimented with farcical techniques.

Farce involves *intensified* body energy. Webster's defines *farce* as "a light dramatic composition marked by *broadly* satirical comedy and improbable plot". Characters take themselves over seriously, and the characterizations are big, wild. There is a lot of business, with an emphasis on *physical* characterization and execution. The energy is more overt than in regular comedy. The danger in farce is that the characters may appear unmotivated. "It is therefore essential to find the heart of the character and keep it always in mind for the truth of what is happening while one is slipping on the banana peel," according to the aforementioned Ms. Seyler.

> In farce, *timing* is everything. I almost choreographed our card game scene, rather than staged it, making sure that each play of cards was precise so that the moves were logical and honest, yet the humor would be in the right place. I had to be sure that farce didn't become burlesque—the latter has no basis in reality or characterization. As we came closer to the opening, these scenes became less farcical and more naturalistic as we found that farce didn't fit into the rest of the production's style. Instead, I asked that all tingle inside with joy but be truthful outside.

Stage Fights—How We Did Them!

Fanny had one scene that required a wild brawl. Staging fight scenes is a skill that has rightly been taken on by specialists. Were this a Shakespearian play, requiring a sword fight, I would have called in a trained combat specialist. If you need such guidance and/or a price list, contact The Society of American Fight Directors, c/o Richard Raether, Fight Masters Magazine, 1834 Camp Avenue, Rockford, Illinois 61103. The brawl in *Fanny*, however, was manageable. The object of staging a fight scene is, of course, to make it look realistic and dangerous, while making sure that *no one gets hurt.*

I staged (with much help from the choreographer and assistant director) a series of grabs and punches in a step-by-step manner, beginning when a sailor kisses the belly dancer. Each step in the series was rehearsed separately. First came a kiss in which the sailor bent the belly dancer backwards over his knee. Then another sailor tried to grab the belly dancer away from him. Next came a punch from the first sailor to Marius and then to yet another sailor. Each time a punch was thrown with the right hand, the left hand was hitting against the actor's own body. This created the sound of an actual fight. The punches were aimed right past each man's ear into the air and would never connect. But the illusion for the audience would be that the punches were tough. After this part of the fight, a third of the action moved offstage with banging and clanging sounds to create the illusion that the fight was continuing.

I asked the cast to perform the fight in slow motion first. Next, we speeded up to one-half time. Finally, the actors performed at almost full speed and energy. We added three of the ensemble screaming onstage and everyone offstage stomping their feet. This all worked together, giving just the right atmosphere. (Total staging time: about one-and-a-half hours.)

Accents

Accents present a special set of problems. When working with accents, I bring in a coach to be in charge, if the budget permits. If not, ask the cast to use their accents (on and offstage, speaking and singing) from the time they walk in the theatre until the time they leave rehearsal. In this way the accent becomes a part of their persona. The same goes for the performances—the actors need to use the accent backstage as well; this takes them out of their own world and puts them into the world of the play. This can really be fun, if entered into with spirit. It's not easy, but it *is* productive.

Tonal "pitch" is very important to complete accent work. The late movie star Peter Sellars understood this; that's why his Inspector Clouseau was so amusing yet believable. (See *Dialects for the Stage,* Theatre Arts Books, 1975, in Recommended Reading.)

For our production of *Fanny* we decided *not* to use French accents, just clear, American English.

Helping Singers to Age Realistically!

A system similar to the one used for accents can be applied to portraying old age or youth. Many musicals contain flashbacks, so these age changes must become part of the actor/singer's psyche and kept in the forefront of consciousness. If the character the singer is playing is old, obviously he or she must work at what is to be "mature" from the very first rehearsal. Once again, as with accents, I have the actors explore and behave and speak in the age of the character from the moment they arrive at rehearsal or at a performance until the moment they leave—the age factor will become instinctive and easy to recreate each time. This was most helpful to the two men playing the fathers.

In this way the values of the scene will come out without what I call the acted "age encumberment" because all have stopped worrying about age and are free to concentrate on the *action* of the scene. We used this system in *Fanny* for Act II rehearsals, in which all were 17 years older.

Improvs can work well in this kind of situation, because using their own words in a scene will help the cast get the age into their bodies. This makes it easier to relax, and to use a true age quality onstage, not a manufactured one.

Frequently, the books of musicals are not written chronologically. If that is the case, take the scenes that are out of context, put them in chronological order, and then have one or two rehearsals in this order, starting from the youngest and going to the oldest. This helps the company to get a feeling of continuity for their characters' lifespan.

Aging Americans and Theatre

You've read and heard about the aging trend in this country, but have you given thought to what this means to your theatre company?

According to a new book, *Age Wave: The Challenges and Opportunities of an Aging America*, by Ken Dychtwald and Joe Flower (Jeffrey Tarcher, Inc.), marketers must take into account the following trends:

- The over-65 population has multiplied three times as fast as the population as a whole.
- The number of Americans over 65 continues to grow by about one-half million each year.

Ask what does this mean to your theatre?

It means looking at your mature audience potential, your current audience and analyzing how to attract this audience for the future of your theatre.

Do you have group rates for the retired? Do you count on their participation as audience? It's a big market!

Usually the seniors group can provide transportation to and from your theatre. You might try to tie in with a local restaurant to include dinner so as to make the evening a special outing.

A group I worked with makes two of their performances into a dinner theatre and provides food at a nominal cost. These performances are always sold out!

Many theatres find their audience dying out because they only work recruiting subscribers—not searching out new audiences.

I refer you to my book "Audience Development and Service" in the *Theatre for the Community* Series published in 1981 by Penn State University for many more practical tips on bringing new people into your theatre.

There is an excellent study program at the University of Nevada Las Vegas (UNLV), called Senior Adult Theatre. It is unique in that it offers a career possibility in the theatre with strong employment opportunities—as the retired population is growing faster than any other in the U.S.

UNLV hosts an annual conference in conjunction with this program, "Senior Theatre USA," bringing together experts in the field. For information write the University of Nevada, Department of Theatre Arts, Las Vegas, Nevada 89154-1001 or attend the conference as it will be an eye opener and help you bring a large, new paying audience into your theatre.

Be sure not to forget the other part of the syndrome—the young! They must be courted and targeted similarly.

More Production Meetings

Our weekly follow-up production meetings bolstered the camaraderie and productivity of the crew. As you get closer to the opening, you must begin to see tangible samples of progress, of course; and that the SM and the crew heads are delegating authority, so the schedule is maintained.

I bring the production meetings up again to remind you to stay in touch with your crew heads and designers. Obviously, the musical director and the choreographer are with you during a good portion of the rehearsals, but your crew people are out doing what they're supposed to be doing (props, costumes, etc.). So at each meeting, I asked what problems they were having and if they needed any help solving them. Usually they didn't, and all seemed to be on schedule.

We all ended up bringing treats to these meetings, and the director gained five pounds.

Microphones

A reminder. If you use mikes, the cast must rehearse with them early on. The company will quickly find they cannot turn toward the wings or the mike level will drop—also, you will find some of your blocking may need redoing in duets to keep sound level even. If you can avoid it, do not use mikes. They are expensive and a big pain. If they are necessary, find someone who has experience with them to guide you.

We did not use mikes in *Fanny*, as it was a small theatre.

Orchestra Rehearsals

Orchestra rehearsals are usually hectic because of lack of sufficient time for musicians and singers to work together. Our musical director had several rehearsals with orchestra separate from our cast. Then for six (long) hours, she joined the orchestra with singers and vice versa. Fine work here and not a minute wasted; so much accomplished in so short a time. As I said in the introduction the theatre is magical (sometimes).

Update and Relaxers

Sharing biographies, animal characterizations, improvising, straight talk, silly moments, new characterization, and passionate feelings all helped the discomfort among the cast to give way. A special kind of trust was developing, and most had become more open and communicative. HURRAY!

Yet, blocking the ensemble into parts of the play that had been previously done with the leads only turned out to be an exhausting task. Many of the ensemble were temporarily bewildered—due to inexperience.

We discovered a blocking error as eight members of the ensemble appeared all from one side of the stage for the song, "Why Be Afraid to Dance." I quipped, "Nobody but an idiot would have staged it that way!" I hastily proceeded to reorganize the entrance.

Exercise

Here is an exercise that helped the cast relax at this tense time and to have fun: I asked that all participate, in pairs. A hands-on, *no talking*, on-your-feet experience. "In the United States we shake hands to greet people (DO IT); on Mars we rub elbows; to say hello on Venus we rub knees." (They continue to do it.) By now, the cast is usually laughing, but they are also looking at one another and *touching* one another. Next they rub behinds, as they do on Jupiter (or Uranus if you dare [sorry]), and then everyone changes partners (and repeats). By the time we've spent ten minutes with this, many inhibitions have been broken down and the laughter has had the desired effect of helping all to experience togetherness. Not a moment too soon because we were about to have a . . .

Run Through

A run through is usually an eye opener, and ours was no exception. We previously had runs of either Act I or Act II but never on the same day. I allowed four hours—and called the entire cast and crew heads. Later, we jokingly called it our *stumble-through!* Here are some sample notes.

Notes

To Panisse: Remember that age is an inner experience and feeling, so it has to come from your center (spine).

To Honorine: Make certain that your character's speaking voice is truthful and in character. Sopranos must speak like people, not like singers.

To Marius: Remember that your character, like most people in real life, has a sense of humor.

To Panisse: There can be much more of a contrast in your ages between Act I and Act II. In Act I, you should be much more youthful, zingier, and full of energy. When you're younger, you're a little more insecure. This insecurity leads you to try harder and that will give you more vigor.

To Fanny: Put a piece of *yourself* into each scene. In each of your love scenes with Marius, feel it deeper and discover what's going on underneath. Don't be afraid of your own passion.

Ensemble: Listen, then react. Learn your cues!

All: What you are doing is adequate—can you find something special? To be or not to be, that is the question—it is also the *answer* in acting a song. *Be*, don't pretend.

I cautioned the entire company that in case they thought they could let up on their efforts because they were doing better (and they were), they couldn't, as I would not have the time to work with them with this intensity once we began teching. (Teching is the time in rehearsal, usually the last week, when you're onstage with cast and crew all working together for the first time.) All of the fine

Most Happy Fella, **Mark Twain Masquers, Hartford, CT. Ann T. Roberts, benefactor. Directed by the author.**

shadings of the characters should come *now,* because soon my energies would be split and devoted also to lights, sound, costumes, etc.

I reiterated that each character's first entrance is very important. That's when the audience decides if they believe who you are and if they like you. Fanny, at this point, was entering a little too coyly and would need to find a more tomboyish and wholesome quality.

The assistant director requested that the ensemble stop focusing on their feet; they looked like "grape crushers"—"Stand still, look up, and play the action. Let me see your eyes!" she said.

We reminded the cast that when there is laughter in the audience, they must pause, breathe in, relax, and then go on, speaking into the very last part of the laugh (with more energy). Feel the flow of enjoyment from the audience, yet *stay in character.*

Further questions arose in my mind as to whether to place the two short vignettes (little scenes) in front of the proscenium curtain (to help with speed of scene changes); and whether to cut a sofa and add a small table stage left (SL) to bring the action farther downstage (DS) and to unclutter things. After experimenting, we did both, bringing the action closer to the audience.

After the run, the director pow-wowed with the creative team. Our conclusions were that the production was slow at the opening and in getting to the climax at the end of Act I. Also, the pace or forward movement of Act II was static, so we would definitely need to find higher stakes for the singer/actor motivations.

My work, for now, would focus on enlarging company energy and moving the musical forward so that the pacing had no unnecessary pauses.

6

Pacing, Blending, Streamlining

Pace is a *major problem* with *most productions* at this stage! Pace is determined by the energy of the cast and the intensity of the interaction—*not just by talking or singing louder or dancing faster*. The way to achieve good pace is to pick up the next line with energy and not a hair's breadth between them. Therefore, the cast must listen and react internally to an action when it happens *before* their cues to eliminate any reaction pauses between lines; if you think about it, this is how *we react in life!* Each scene has a pace because of the emotions of the participants. Individual reactions cause others to give (and take), and can help the pace and energy of a scene *without unwanted pauses*.

> ### Exercise
>
> When the pace is bogged down, start with the troubled pages, and have the cast say the lines while running in place (like jogging). Exhausting, yes—but effective in bringing up their energy level and forcing the cast to LISTEN (when they stop laughing).
>
> If you have soft-spoken singers who seem to be underplaying, ask them to shout their lines *passionately* across the room for two minutes, forcing them to use their bodies and lift their energy (and projection). In our production I used this many times with our young leads and with the ensemble.

So pace is an intermingling of many things—actors, director, moods—all of these combined with the author's words to create a level of energy. What can happen is that the director might forget his/her thoughts on the original values and allow the singers to lessen the established interaction. This is not productive as it slows things down. Many times, when pace is too slow, the clue is that the company's emotions are too one-dimensional and there is a need to ask the group to deepen and re-examine individual reactions and raise their involvement and stakes in the scene or song. By doing this the emotions then deepen further and push the others to stronger reactions.

Pauses, How to Eliminate the Unwanted Ones

Exercise

In spite of using what I've just outlined, many were still having trouble picking up their cues fast enough (with the result that there were pauses, which slowed the pace). So we tried this: All were asked to please speak his/her first word on the previous character's last word—Marius speaks *into* the last word of Caesar's sentence, Honorine speaks *on* the last word of Panisse's sentence, etc. (They had to overlap because in order to do this exercise you "super" listen which causes an energy reaction to flow through the body eliminating most pauses.) Suddenly, we eliminated 30 or more unwanted pauses. Truly, this exercise not only helped the interaction and therefore the pace but also forced all to *listen* or get left out.

One unwanted pause occurred again in a scene in Act II, when Marius motioned to the stairs and asked Fanny, "What's up there?" Fanny paused, ran to the stairs, stretched her arms out to block his passage and finally said, "Just the bedrooms." Of course, her motive was to protect her son Cesario from seeing Marius, but the long pause between "What's up there?" and "Just the bedrooms," was not only odd but unreal.

I explained to Fanny that she must experience it first in her brain before it would translate into emotion (heart) and action (body). The internal response for "Just the bedrooms," would therefore occur immediately, *as* she ran to block him on the stairs. The run to the stairs could occur as she was saying the line, thus eliminating the pause.

The next unwanted pause occurred in a moment before Marius kissed Fanny. They were speaking to each other from a distance of about a foot, forcing Marius to step in to kiss Fanny. Instead, I moved the two lovers tightly together. If Marius would say his lines that close to Fanny, and with passion, the kiss would come as a natural progression of events, rather than after a pause. In other words, there would be nothing for Fanny and Marius to do *but* kiss. We later used this technique in the title song, their big love duet, named (of course) "Fanny."

In Act II, in the scene where Panisse is being helped into the room and onto the chaise, Fanny tells him to lie down. The timing of the scene, however, had Panisse pausing at the chaise long before Fanny had a chance to tell him to lie down. "If the dialogue moves fast enough and you walk slowly enough," I told them, "and if the gods are with us, it will work—*help one another.*"

Special Rehearsal

A request was made for use of the stage for one rehearsal a week and a half before we were to move onstage, in order to familiarize the company with the actual layout of the theatre and auditorium. Since the cast would make entrances and exits from the aisles and floor of the theatre, as well as through the side doors and steps to the stage, I thought it important that they walk through their blocking to time entrances and exits. With a group this large, and with a rehearsal space that did not quite measure the actual size of the stage and with the unusual entrances we had blocked (many through the aisles), an early, onstage rehearsal was a necessity. So we took the plunge and tried an *onstage* walk/run-through with rehearsal props and some of the costumes, as the costume designer wanted all to be aware of and get used to fast changes. First reactions:

Messy and just okay! Our musical director complained that, as I had blocked several scenes on the apron, she could not see or hear singers through the front curtain (the orchestra was offstage left). My suggestion, that we could remedy this by using a scrim (see glossary) in place of the curtain, satisfied her well enough but posed yet another problem for the set crew, as the only scrim available had to be pulled by hand and needed two people to do so. But it did help, so it was worth the extra effort.

Viewing the group even in partial costume, for the first time, was a delight. Fanny, who often wore a plain black rehearsal skirt, was dressed in a charming

French milkmaid's costume, pure and white. With her hair covered with a cap, her real age of 27 melted to 17.

Panisse and Cesar changed from their rehearsal pants or jeans into dapper men-about-town suits with straw hats and canes.

Ensemble members were still depending on the person next to them to carry the song. Afraid of hitting the wrong note, the first note of each ensemble song was never sung cleanly. As a result, the music director and I scheduled a music rehearsal for confidence-building (using one of my "trouble-spot" (TBA) rehearsal times).

By midnight I felt we had rehearsed past the time of profit and sent the cast home. It was well worth all the effort, as we were able to see so many things that would make our work stronger and more focused. As you know, until you actually see the production onstage, it's in your mind's eye only. What this run-through did was to help me clearly see what was working and what was not.

Sorting Out

Honorine had found a new prop, a sexy black fan, which she used both to attract admirers and shoo away detractors. Good, good. In the "Never Too Late" musical number, Honorine and Panisse make playful fun of Cesar, who is readying himself for what he believes to be a secret rendezvous. I tried to capture the *essence* of the *relationship* of the three characters to each other. Cesar becomes furious with the two for teasing him; Panisse gains a point in his game of one-upsmanship with Cesar; and Honorine pokes Panisse away with her fan because he failed to propose to her. They were wonderful here, and I *remembered* to *say so*!!!

Fanny has a scene with the old Admiral in which she is supposed to come storming in. Unfortunately, our Fanny played the scene too gently, instead of with the spunkiness that would make her character more believable and likeable. We went over (and over), trying new variations, until she found the courage to give way to necessary feelings of passion. This was a rehearsal in which, as I later felt during my "think time", I had wasted energy repeating rather than trying new exercises or improvs. I would not do that again, as time is precious.

The last song and scene of *Fanny* is most interesting below the surface (subtext). The plot is simply that Panisse is dying. The situation, dialogue, and the final song are, indeed, quite sad. The fascinating thing during rehearsal was that the more heavily and tragically the two characters played the scene, the less sad those of us who experienced the song became, so the assistant director suggested to me that

I ask the actors to counter the plot line by being irreverent, continuing to play their one-upsmanship rather than playing the somber mood of impending death. This reversal, which focused on the continued normal relationship between the two men (playing *subtext*), made the characters poignant yet funny. Thanks for assistant directors and collaboration! (Subtext is explored in a most original way as "Biological Self" and "Social Self" in Moni Yakim's fascinating book, *Creating a Character* [for advanced work].)

Still digesting my notes and the suggestions of the designers, crew heads, and creative staff from the onstage run-through, I took stock of our production. First of all, we needed to start trimming bits and pieces that weren't working and probably never would work. This would cut minutes at least, and was done with no fuss, easily and quickly. Our next task would be focused on blending the show, so that the flow from book to song to dance would become seamless. That is what would make it look effortless on opening night—the big picture. In addition, we had to continue work on concentration.

At the next rehearsal we spent three hours going from musical numbers to book sections and vice versa, until we had gone through blending the entire show. I asked that lights and sound be with us so they too could see the work cut out for them at the next rehearsals; blending all—cast and crew—would be crucial.

Here is something to remind you of how to continue this important *process of evaluation*: ("Need" (energy) as used here is comparable to what Stanislavski calls *motivation*, or objectives.)

Instead of just trying to sing it better or faster or something, you can say, "Aha! Obviously the song we have put together in this way (or are singing in such-and-such a way, or the scene we have designed, or the dance we have choreographed) to project the need energy, is malfunctioning." And you go back and look at that. Instead of firing the choreographer or screaming about the poster or blaming the lighting designer, you go back and deal with *your* text interpretation, which is almost always where the problem is. And you re-analyze the text to find out why what you have on the stage is not doing what the score and the text need it to do.

Ask yourself what the problem can be. Is the song itself just an unsatisfactory piece of music? Is it the lyric that's not clear? Or is it not being delivered properly? Maybe the performer has made a wrong choice in terms of the quality she's trying to project. Is it the orchestration? Sometimes, for example, the orchestration might be inappropriate. Maybe the orchestration is putting up a barrier. Or maybe it's the costuming. Maybe there's something about the way she's dressed at that time that makes her look too finished and too lacquered. Maybe the costume and hairdo need a looser, more vulnerable quality, so that the audience can see her. It could be one or all of those factors, or a whole bunch more. *But understanding the proper* flow of energies in the *show* tells you where to look. It's not hard analysis to do. But in the excitement of getting the show on, too many people forget to do it. The ones who remember usually turn out good shows. (Charlie Willard, quoted by David Ball in *Teaching Theatre Magazine.*)

Look to the source—you, *the director.*

To clarify further, here are the same thoughts but with a different viewpoint: written to the me by Dr. Ronald Willis of the University of Kansas, Lawrence, after reading an earlier manuscript of this book.

There is one thing I'd like to suggest you consider focusing on a bit more. I suppose it comes under the heading of Script Analysis, but it has actorly implications as well. It is the simple direction to look for the moments when a *discovery* is made or a *decision* is reached. Another way to say it is to ask the director and the cast to look for the irreversible moments, those places where action or consciousness (either the character's, the audience's, or the story) reaches new plateaus and so cannot be turned back or neutralized. If more directors and actors paid attention to the *unfolding nature* of the play's contained consciousness, I would be happier as an audience member. I would get to see real progression in productions that now only attitudinize about a static issue. If all the creative agents would then look to ways of increasing the contrast between the times before and after each of those decision/discovery/turning points, I would be in theatre heaven.

Plugging Along: Then Disaster

Due to a last-minute mix-up (the polite word) in scheduling, this became a rehearsal without a pianist.

Disaster struck! It was fiasco time.

Our stage manager was not able to prompt because he was breaking in his brand-new assistant stage manager. And our assistant director, who would normally fill in, was ill.

The man playing Escartifique was drafted to play the piano, and he did so with a tortuous lack of ease, never having played the music before. The burden on him of jumping in to say his lines and jumping out to play the accompaniment was obvious (my mistake).

As if this were not enough confusion, a new prop assistant, at rehearsal for only the second time, was continually running in with questions.

My nerves were already frayed, and all this did little to help. Concentration was of course not fully there, making things worse, if possible.

Marius and the Admiral played their whole scene hidden behind a new bench. What is it about the furniture that makes cast members seek refuge behind it?

In another scene, with nine people onstage, a pause occurred. Everyone's eyes shot up toward the stage manager, as each person thought he/she was the one guilty of forgetting a line. Later I mentioned the great stage star Lynn Fontanne's famous supposed response to a telephone that rang by mistake in the middle of a scene with her co-star (and offstage husband), Alfred Lunt. She paused and gracefully walked to the phone, calmly picked up the receiver, listened, smiled, and said, "It's for you." It's called *concentration!* Concentration is the state of being connected; united.

Concentration: The Dustin Hoffman Story

This brings to mind one of my favorite true stories. I had the pleasure of hosting Dustin Hoffman and driving him to a theatre conference. He was appearing at the Kennedy Center in *Death of a Salesman* and had agreed to come and speak to about 200 theatre people about acting.

Characteristically, I managed to take a wrong turn and get us temporarily lost. I quickly got back on the right road, which amused Mr. Hoffman and his companions a good deal and did make our time together more relaxed.

I had the honor of introducing him. He came onstage to much applause and was low-key at first. He started by talking about playing Willy Loman and then about acting in the movies. He proceeded to talk for several hours. It was fascinating, a tender, beautiful experience. One of the things I'd been so impressed with the several times I'd seen him play Willy was his absolute power of *concentration*. Nothing deterred him from his focus, drive, and characterization. He was the same way as he spoke to the group, getting so involved in exploring acting techniques the hours passed quickly and the time to leave came too soon.

The musical, *Chicago*, University of Florida, photo by Albert F. C. Wehlburg.

Getting him back was my responsibility (having been told to make sure he returned to the Kennedy Center on time or it might be wise to look for other work). I had pre-arranged a signal with him: when it was time to go, I would unobtrusively stand up.

So I did. There I was, several minutes later, still standing, and he was still talking. I tried to get his attention without distracting the crowd, which was clearly enraptured. Finally I thought, "Well, there goes my wonderful job." So I said, "Mr. Hoffman!" He went right on. I shouted, "Dustin Hoffman!" He looked at me and said, "Oh, yes David." He'd been so concentrated on what he wanted to say that he had not heard me before. I said, "I know you want to make your matinee, and it's important that I bring you back, and on time." He smiled and concluded in three or four minutes.

The end of the story is that I did get him back in time, but we laughed that he still might be talking if I hadn't been able to get his attention and break his concentration.

My point here is that being connected (concentrated) is of the utmost importance to any song or scene. So share this story with your cast and then use the next two exercises to help.

Exercise

Concentration

Ask your cast to improvise the following scenes (or make up your own to go with your production):

1. Two lovers preparing to commit suicide on top of the Empire State Building. One of their mothers arrives and tries to take her offspring home.

2. A man and woman meet in a public park after 14 years. A policeman comes and insists that they leave.

Concentrate on the task at hand in spite of distractions.

Videotaping Could Help

One colleague has found that a videotape of the entire musical (or scenes from it), made about two-and-a-half weeks into rehearsal, is an excellent tool to help the cast see who is concentrating, who is making pauses. When the tape is played back, both the director and the group can see clearly who and what is working. Those in the cast who perhaps haven't been able to feel or understand their part or what the director is trying to get out of them can see they are lagging behind, and they need to adjust and *do something*. This director feels it is particularly helpful in songs during which the characters' bodies don't seem to be doing what they should. Since singers can't see themselves in rehearsal, if they can watch what they are doing, or rather, *not* doing on the tape, it does enlighten. Taping can also be used when the singers are working with accents or playing old age—they can hear and see themselves as you see them. See previous sections on Accents and Aging Realistically, in Chapter 5.

Some directors abhor this taping technique. Personally, I'm on the fence —it really depends on the company. Yet I do think in a musical number that it can help you (the director) and the cast see instantly what is working, what needs redoing, and who is not up to par with the rest of the company.

Publicity and Photographs— Necessary Interruptions

The cast was scheduled to have publicity photographs taken at 1:00 p.m. sharp— the photographer had another appointment and could not be detained (since he was donating his services). Many of the leads, who had rehearsed lines on their own all that morning, arrived at the last minute to change for the photographs. In the midst of this, the cast of the show currently playing in the theatre was using the costume room, preparing for a matinee performance. Consequently, our costumer was unable to use the costume room, and had to dress the tardy actors in the hall and rehearsal room.

Marius, who had gotten his times mixed up, never showed for the photo session, so I had no choice but to stage the photo session without him: Cesar and Panisse on a bench, Honorine patting Cesario's head using her wonderful fan, Fanny swinging around an old-fashioned lamp-post, Panisse holding Fanny's hand. These handsome 8x10 black-and-white stills would be sent to newspapers to publicize the show. They would also be in the packets handed to critics when they came to review the show. Publicity is a necessary tool in theatre and has to be dealt with—it's part of the director's responsibility, to help facilitate this process.

7

Onstage—Finally

Light/Sound, Dry Tech

I sat out front and was given a cue-to-cue look at sound and lights. Cue to cue means going from first light and sound cue to next to next, etc., to last one, including the curtain call without actor/singers or dialogue to set the technical aspects of the show. The assistant director and the stage manager walked through all blocking to make sure I could *see* what, when, and where I needed to. We made adjustments, up, down (for intensity), out/in (for space), lights off walls onto faces, etc. Follow spot operators, who had rehearsed previously with large flashlights, were almost perfect.

Then the stage manager and light board operator went over each cue so that at the next light run-through with the cast, we would have as few glitches and stops as possible. Naturally, this *would be adjusted* up to and through the previews. We added *blue* lights backstage for the actors and orchestra. This made it possible for the cast and crew to see and move backstage during blackouts, yet the light would not be seen from the audience.

Sound was added to our tech to set volume and length only, as I had previously heard all the sound cues. They were fine, adding just the atmosphere we wanted.

After ten hours we were exhausted but organized—crew, designers, as well as the director, stage manager, and assistant director, knowing much could go wrong at the next rehearsal (and would), but not for lack of preparation. All this would require fine-tuning at each of the subsequent rehearsals, but *Fanny was teched.*

(It turned out that the light and sound changes and adjustments were only necessary in 15 percent of cues.)

Rehearsal with Sets, Costumes, and Tech

Well, here we finally were onstage for good. At last!! The SM walked the cast around the sets and backstage setup. I told the cast and crew I would not stop the action for any reason. Once full dress rehearsals start, the director, in effect, hands over the reins to the stage manager, who henceforth runs the show. Silently, I readied my pad and pencil, prepared to take voluminous notes, and I did, of course!

While concentrating on continuity and adjusting to sets, lights, and costumes, the cast tended to lose many of the emotional moments. The scenes that we had rehearsed most successfully, and those songs that had been in the best shape in recent rehearsals were weak. Dances that had come together before, amazingly, were diffused.

During the "intermission" the actors discussed their mistakes and plotted to improve.

Because it was so late when the final curtain came down, I decided to save specific notes until the next day, but I had some brief thoughts for all.

The show had run fairly well, but it did not flow together—it seemed long; the scene changes were ragged. Songs were strong, but the blend into (and out of) them still took too much time!

We discussed pauses (again!) Ones that allow an audience to absorb an emotional moment, for instance, are fine, and, if used judiciously, are dramatically exciting. However, when rendered in excess, and for no reason, they can be killing to the forward movement of the show. Pauses due to an actor forgetting a line or letting down the energy level can ruin the timing and flow of a scene as well. We always wanted the production to stay ahead of the audience, I reminded.

The next day, I gave individual notes as the cast was putting on makeup. Here are a few as examples:

To Cesar: "Last evening *you* enjoyed your song 'I Like You' so much that you were no longer acting the song, only impersonally involved in singing it." I reminded him that the audience would nod off if he failed to *feel* as well as sing.

To Escartifique: "You faked being drunk half of the time, instead of really being it." I reminded him that someone who is drunk is trying his best not to look like a fool or like he's drunk.

We used the next exercise with immediate results.

> ### Exercise
>
> "Please, just do this one action—try to appear sober so as not to be embarrassed in front of your friends—and express that in your own words," I said. He did, two times, and then went back to the authors' words, and it made quite a difference. He wasn't pretending to be drunk but playing his action through subtext. And to make things even better, the other cast members reacted strongly, as this time he was so true to life, and their reactions, in turn, helped him.

More Observations

An ensemble member entirely missed the cue for her one scene. Lines were lost. Nervous singers reverted to old song blocking, which had long since been changed. The actress playing Honorine fell off one of the unanchored bales in mid-song and fortunately was caught by her fellow cast members. (To her credit, she continued without a break.) The final scenes between Cesar and Panisse in Act II dragged unmercifully—and had been so touching in previous rehearsals.

The piano had hammered away, drowning out dialogue and the singers' voices. The set change from Act I to Act II had required exhausting maneuvering (and time).

Yet, in spite of all this, much was affecting, moving, and almost fun.

Some Breakthroughs

I had to try to soften some of the remaining theatrical mannerisms in order to make the scenes more true to life. In the love scene I asked Marius just to talk to Fanny in a normal voice and tell her he loved her. The magic that Marius thought he was creating by sexy whispering was changed when he stopped acting so much and just allowed himself to enjoy the atmosphere and a lovely girl's company.

In my efforts to get to the honesty and compassion between mother and daughter (Fanny and Honorine), I began to talk too loud and feel edgy. The actor/singer playing the mother became more frustrated and confused, and I

An amusing
publicity shot
of a rehearsal.

became impatient. Later I felt I had been too hard on her, thereby confusing her further. My gut feeling was that whatever she was doing was simply because she didn't understand—so we started again. "Forget everything you planned at home; just do it—experience the other characters," I said. "Don't tell Fanny what to do; focus on what you are doing. Give in to the moment—don't plan now. FEEL."

At long last the scene started to work. "Is that what you want?" Honorine asked, as her fight against herself caved in. Yes! A real breakthrough! After hugs we did the scene again—PROGRESS! Since she was doing so well and allowing herself to be vulnerable, it seemed a good time to work on her solo, even though it was not on the agenda. We did, and she was on target, singing from the heart!!

Fanny's line to Marius after his fight with Panisse was, "What made you do that Marius?" I told her, "You play-acted your jealousy, sounding coy. Can you let go? Remember your own youth and BECOME Fanny, the young girl! Try this."

Exercise

I asked that she skip around the room, saying in her own words what Fanny's inner feelings (subtext) were out loud, which she did with gusto. Then I asked her to go back to her dialogue with this same passion, and it worked. Many reviewers singled her out for joyous, youthful, realistic characterization.

Perhaps because I was coming down with a cold, or perhaps because of my awareness that time was growing short, I felt exhausted by the cast, overwhelmed by the show. The days were slipping by and my work with the group would all too quickly be over. The need to work out those final problems kept me up a good part of the night, making me think harder of ways to *help* rather than *blame.*

The set, which had been improving day by day thanks to a new paint job and details added by the set decorators, was looking more three dimensional. You could still see some of the braces of the flats from the audience, so they would need to be painted black, of course. Meanwhile, our trusted stage manager was distributing more crew and design notes.

Fine-Tuning the Songs

In the middle of the next working rehearsal, I joked: "There must be a plot to put Cesar behind someone!" as I rushed from the audience up the stairs and onto the stage. Every time Cesar sang onstage, he wound up behind someone or something.

"You're hedging all over the place. If you are supposed to cross to the gate, then cross and be there. I can't see or feel that you love this village!"

We redid the song to help him to stand *still,* and cut some of my favorite blocking to do it. The point was to help the man be comfortable in order to let him do his best work. I asked that he see what he was singing about with his inner eye. As he allowed his feelings to come out and to show via the lyric, his body relaxed and this ended up one of my favorite numbers in our production.

So *never* give up—and neither you nor the cast should be afraid of last-minute changes.

The music director still had concerns about Panisse's song, "Never Too Late"; it was his first one in the show. Instead of tensing up as he began to sing, he needed to charm. "How do you charm?" we asked. Tease, enjoy—flirt with the females. He tried and actually amused himself, so it worked, because that action took his mind off of himself and doing a good job and focused it on the situation to have fun and enjoy his friends.

Interestingly, just as the woman playing Honorine had finally stopped directing herself during her scenes, the man playing Marius also began to relax. The evening before, I had told him not to criticize himself as he went along—just stay in character (thereby letting his own considerable personal warmth come through Marius).

I complimented the ensemble, who now looked like they might make it. The show couldn't work without all pulling their own weight, and it was apparent that everyone was really concentrating.

The changes made may have seemed small, but these moments of truth would stay in the hearts of the audience long after they had forgotten the evening's entertainment.

Last Dress Rehearsals—Progress

Our hairdresser had been working with Honorine, who had tried on a red, frowsy wig for Act I and a more stylish and subdued wig for Act II (to show her change in status to a rich mother-in-law). He had pulled Fanny's hair every which way, testing out different styles and working with braided hairpieces to achieve the sophistication needed for Act II. (The wigs we'd chosen just didn't look real, so we returned them.)

I reminded the harried costumer to dirty up the fishermen's clothes more so they would look realistic and not like musical costumes.

This was our most hectic time—we call it "hell week"—though you all know nothing can adequately describe it!

There was applause for the costume designer as the actors got together in full dress. She reminded the actors to bathe each night (the men, to wear undershirts and undershorts) to protect their costumes.

I sat in the audience at a table with the lighting and sound designers. We communicated through headsets wired to the sound/lighting booth and to the stage manager's table backstage. In this way corrections could be made immediately. If the sound cues were not loud enough, or the lights not set at the proper level, an adjustment could then be made without interfering with the action onstage or distracting the actors.

We did a run of the show. In fact, we ran Act II *first.* (A good idea, so high energy can be channeled into Act II and not always into Act I.)

Exercise

At the intermission, all were exhausted, so I asked everyone in the cast to lie on the floor or sit in a chair with their backs well supported and close their eyes and to try to have as few thoughts in their minds as possible and just concentrate on saying the "ohm" (om) sound to themselves to relax. After eight minutes, energy seemed to be restored, so we changed costumes and the set and proceeded. This is a type of meditation technique that most found helpful.

Before every rehearsal we sat still for four to five minutes. This helps the group forget about the day's problems and channels the positive energy into the rehearsal. Jean Sabatine in her fine book *Actors Image* (Backstage Books, 1994) explores this further with a fascinating technique called *loosening the chakras,* using the mind, spirit, and body as thought, emotion, and action.

The dress rehearsal was sloppy. One dancer lost her skirt during "Why Be Afraid To Dance," and the Admiral had trouble remembering his lines. Cesario's makeup made him look suddenly and curiously as if he were from outer space. Fanny, in a tight dress, and Brun, the second lead, in a nightshirt, gave accidental showings of their underwear as they knelt in Act II. One spotlight seemed obstinate in its refusal to fall directly on the faces of Marius and Fanny, but below their waists.

I empathized with the ensemble, who had to sit in the wings or dressing room for lengthy periods and then appear for only a few moments with a great burst of energy, which made their jobs more difficult, possibly, than the leads.

As messy as the dress rehearsal had been, the show was coming along. And we still had four more days to make it stronger! Keeping the production moving with no stage waits from songs to book and light cue to light cue was the problem. Crews were still in early rehearsal, and actor/singers were just getting used to crews and vice versa.

Congratulations were definitely in order for the crews and SM—well done with so little tech rehearsal time. Half a miracle. There was a heightened feeling of comraderie and trust amongst the company that vibrated onstage. At this final stage, singer/actors (one hopes) touch one another not only physically and emotionally, but also *spiritually*.

Tomorrow, the orchestra will return! This will help.

Staging the Curtain Calls

Curtain calls are an integral part of any performance; they are the last thing the audience sees before exiting the theatre. A poorly staged curtain call can lessen a fine performance. I staged the calls (two days before first preview), and then each time we rehearsed Act II we rehearsed the calls—bowing all *together*, keeping heads up and smiling. I was careful to give the leads their due, and yet not ignore the ensemble and orchestra.

Preview

During the first public performance, the audience will let you know what's working, where there will be laughter, and what the weak spots are, thus giving you time before the next preview to make adjustments. By opening night, you might even enjoy yourself—well, almost!

At our first preview, we had about a third of a house of invited patrons from a nearby hospital and a group of senior citizens. Slowly (too slowly), laughter filled the auditorium—and there was applause after some of the songs. When the curtain closed on Act I, smiles were on the faces of the crowd and I listened intently to their comments and made notes. Many in the audience spoke about how real the show was ("like our family," one member said).

In Act II when Marius appeared, back from the sea to find Fanny again, an elderly gentleman in the front row cried: "Oh, no, he's back. It's Marius!" It warmed us all.

After the final curtain I sent the cast and crew home with thanks—planning to give lots of individual notes during the hour the cast was putting on makeup the next evening.

Organizing my notes and thoughts at home, I concluded: Seventy percent of the show was quite good; the rest, unfocused and slow. Act I lacked real energy in the first ten minutes because of the male chorus in the opening number. There was still not enough chemistry among the men. We called a special 30-minute rehearsal during which I asked that they listen to each other every minute and let that listening go through their entire bodies. I felt although we didn't really have the time at this stage, we had to try to loosen that number—and get the men to use their *inner energy*.

Exercise

I asked the group (and Marius) to do their opening scene at (almost) double intensity, then again, and to listen/react and speak or sing on the last word of the previous character's line. We did this two times back to back. And it helped, finally!

The drums in the dance scenes needed to come in immediately (and softer) in the darkness after the previous scene. The piano still showed through the scrim and needed a back cover. The electric candle on the bar table in Act I would have to be replaced with a real candle, because it looked fake. The stage manager called to check the local fire code to make sure we could use the real thing. The answer was yes, *if* the tablecloth was fireproofed. (You bet it was, by the next rehearsal.)

The fog machine worked beautifully in creating the Marseilles waterfront atmosphere for the opening of Act I.

Bits and pieces of the delightful and humorous circus choreography were executed beautifully. Bravo to our dancers and choreographer! I was very pleased with the three minutes of trimming the choreographer had done because the show was still running too long.

The Act II climax with Marius's return was flowing with unusual power, and Panisse's death scene was moving to the point of tears. Some of our hard work was paying off.

A number of lines that were letter-perfect at the preceding dress rehearsal were now being paraphrased. The SM had notes on line paraphrases and gave them to the cast and would continue to do so.

David Young
with Jason
Robards at a
Kennedy Center
workshop.

The curtain call worked, and the actors joined in for a brief reprise of "Panisse and Son" after their bows. (We needed to soften the sad ending and send the audience home humming.)

Opening Night

Just as the set seemed to "become" Marseilles, so did the cast seem to "become" their characters. Their stage names began to fit them more, and their everyday lives in the workaday world seemed to disappear. Laughter filled the auditorium; applause was appreciative.

When the company appeared for the finale, they were beaming. Knowing they had touched the audience, they "ate up" the applause. They left the theatre for the party to celebrate. I was pleased and I shared that with all (cast and crew).

The next day most of the reviews corroborated this.

Evaluation

Reviews or no reviews, it was a realized work— the best all could do for now. It is fine to receive good notices, but there are other ways and standards by which to evaluate. The judgment of trusted professionals, as well as your audience, tells the true story.

My own honest critics—mentors, colleagues—had enjoyed the show, but made suggestions for improvement. (They came at my request the previous week to help me see the strengths and weaknesses more clearly.)

The reviewers commented that the evening was more like a play with music than a musical. In a number of reviews the critics had referred to the cast singing so well in character. Unfortunately, some of the reviewers commented unfavorably on the ensemble—yet they had worked so hard.

We arranged for a rehearsal after opening night, to tighten the production, as the audience had been our final collaborator. As one performance gave way to the next, small errors popped up along the way. One night the fog-maker refused to work. On another night, the fog worked so well that it was two to three minutes into the scene before the audience could see the actors on stage. Another night, Honorine's fish cart/bike became tangled with the wire on the stage manager's headset. Honorine continued onstage as she undauntedly untangled the wire from the wheel—the audience roared their approval.

At this point a director knows full well it is too late to make changes. Just let the cast and audience mix; the director needs to *get out of the way*. Adjustments at this juncture would only confuse. The realization dawns that this is the work for now.

The applause each evening made everything worthwhile—theatre is, after all, a "celebration" for the audience, the cast, and crew.

GOOD LUCK!—and BREAK A LEG with your production! Whatever musical you choose, remember, "The Joy Is in the Doing!" And when you do, you will have . . .

BROADWAY, YOUR WAY.

I

Understanding and Directing Young People and Teens

Dr. Xan S. Johnson

Some Background

My assumption will be that you already know something about directing a play. The purpose of this chapter will be to provide you information that will help you apply your existing directing skills to working with children and young teens. Directing children and young teen actors in plays and musicals cast primarily with adult actors and targeted for a general adult or family audience *is* a different context from directing children and young teens in plays and musicals cast primarily with children or young teen actors and targeted for a young people's audience—usually called Children's Theatre, Young People's Theatre, or Youth Theatre. I will assume most of you work primarily in the adult theatre and cast young people once in a while, hence I will focus on the first set of circumstances, but be reassured that the information is applicable and helpful to both directing situations.

Stanislavski, who opened one of the world's first professional Children's Theatres at the famous Moscow Art Theatre over a century ago, was once asked what the difference was between theatre for children and theatre for adults. "Nothing," replied Stanislavski, "except theatre for children must be a little bit better!" What I think Stanislavski meant by this is that all theatre, regardless of your targeted audience, must share the same high artistic standards, but when the target audience *is* children or young teens, you must go the *extra mile* to learn about the specific needs and characteristics unique to children at different stages of maturation.

For the purposes of our situation, the "extra mile" suggestion also holds true for directors that choose to cast children and young teens in their primarily adult productions. Please remember that each director must eventually create his/her own system of communicating with young actors. There are simply too many variables to set in concrete something called a system for directing young people. However, if you take the time to learn about young people and what makes them tick at certain times of their childhood, you will be able to find something that works for you.

Young people, it is true, do see the same world we adults see, but the way they experience and understand this "same" world is quite different. As I talk with you about young people, I will only be referring to children ages eight through twelve and young teens ages thirteen through fifteen because most children seven and under are high-risk props on stage and generally have little value other than cuteness. Most teens sixteen and older are capable of functioning as adults most of the time. The general rule of thumb in the Children's Theatre profession is beware of casting children under the age of ten in adult theatre projects. "Family Theatre" productions such as *The Sound of Music, Anne Frank,* and *To Kill a Mockingbird* are examples of shows in which you may elect to cast young people if good talent can be found. But even in these modern classics, I do not recommend casting under the age ten if the role has any substance at all. In terms of child development and artistic product, casting younger than ten is not a justifiable risk.

Note

Keep in mind that Stanislavski, often called the father of modern acting, came to the world of theatre from an *opera* background, from *musical theatre,* you might say. He may well have observed the sincere emotional depth opera singers could generate through the release of their vocal performance. In contrast, he was appalled at the "bombastic physicality" employed by most stage actors of his day and at their total rejection of emotional reality. American musicals that focus only on "the musical number" and demand little in the way of emotional depth and reality from actors would, I'm sure, also greatly appall the acting master. I am convinced Stanislavski wanted to see in the stage actor an emotional life as powerfully real as what he had heard in the voice of the opera singer. Hence, we now have the famous Stanislavski actor training system and its many variations and interpretations over the years.

A Little Theory

Critical to understanding children and young teens is your ability to understand the difference between the concept of *performing* and *acting*. *Performing* is the natural, attention-seeking act of self-presentation; performance is, by nature, selfish. A degree of selfishness is essential to human development, even in adulthood, and should not be considered a negative trait under most circumstances. *Acting* is the complex and abstract act of performing a character within the formalized art form called theatre, and, although self-indulgence may be present in it, acting is, by nature, very unselfish in its purest form.

In children and young teens, *performing* is what you get most all of the time. This is true because performing, attention seeking, and highly centered behavior come naturally to all young people. Some, however, are naturally drawn to the theatre's unique brand of attention fulfillment because their personalities have the right combination of traits to make them comfortable and motivated to seek acting experiences rather than what they might find in such other fields as science, athletics, or visual arts.

Many young people wish to "try on" the theatre experience. Many will decide it is not what they expected or simply lose interest and move on. Others may have a tenacious, long-term interest, and/or a legitimate gift in theatre. Most young people, however, are simply demonstrating a natural propensity and comfort with theatre, but are not ready for acting. This in no way prevents them from contributing tremendously to an entertaining and highly artistic production.

Mentally, acting requires abstract thinking or the ability to imagine the ideal character (a mental hypothesis) and integrate that totally independent image into one's own perceived self-image (hypothesis testing) for the purpose of role communication. Children and most young teens *play* roles (*stand for another* through externally selected signs and symbols—seldom any emotional empathy or intimacy present); adults trained in acting *communicate* roles (*become another* through the internal integration of personality aspects from self and others, processed into an externalized whole. Emotional empathy and intimacy should always be present.)

Children under the age of twelve seldom have the capacity for abstract thinking; rather, they plan logical physical choices to present based on concrete thinking where information is gathered through available, hands-on (concrete) sources, e.g., the director, the script, etc. On the stage, they are simply being themselves and presenting a variety of planned attitudes and physicalizations at different levels of understanding and comfort. For the most part, this is performing, not acting.

Children under twelve not only prefer, but actually benefit much more from, *creative drama,* which is defined as a non-audience, role-playing process focused on improvisation and story dramatization for sake of the participants' personal, psychosocial, and/or educational growth. Children *believe* they want to perform and the actual performance before an audience can be rewarding to some degree at whatever stage of development a child might be, however children under twelve most often dislike structured play rehearsals, waiting to work, blocking and polish, many repetitions, etc., especially compared to the autonomy and the spontaneity they experience in creative drama. The more creative drama/improvisation-based your rehearsals can be, the better off you will be.

Young teens, between the ages of thirteen and fifteen, should have the capacity for abstract thought and, therefore, could begin to understand the concept of acting. But often, because of the naturally occurring emotional intensity in their lives caused by raging hormones and a new, decentered view of the world that often temporariliy strips them of their self-esteem, young teens often regress to the earlier stages where they last felt emotionally safe.

Although most young teens would probably choose theatre over creative drama at this age, the use of improvisation in rehearsals is still very popular and important. The good news is that structured play rehearsals are better tolerated and understood by young teens.

Keep in mind that the developmental stages I speak of are not necessarily rigid. You will find exceptions to the rule, individuals ahead of or behind schedule, but such exceptions will often be limited to a very narrow set of skills. Also keep in mind that developmental stages are hierarchical, not mutually exclusive. This means that a child moving from stage three to stage four hierarchically expands or brings with him/her all that he/she learned in stages one, two, and three, in the same way that we all continue to seek attention throughout our lives in one way or another, even though this is a trait most commonly associated with very young children.

So, why cast children or young teens at all? In my sixteen years of directing plays at the university theatre and semiprofessional/community theatre level, *intergenerational casting* has provided the best formula for success and high theatre art. The dynamics created by the dramatic interaction of adults and young people can be deeply moving, spontaneous, and magically rewarding to the audience. I always cast a child role with a child actor whenever I can find a child capable of performing the role. When I cannot find a qualified child at the right age, I cast as young and as small as I can.

Scene from *The Little Match Girl,* directed by Dr. Xan S. Johnson.

Directing Suggestions

Auditions. In Young People's Theatre we have a saying—when you cast a young person in your play you also cast a parent. My *audition form* for young people asks for information above and beyond the form usually used for adult actors. My form includes a request for such things as parent(s)' name(s), address(es), phone numbers at home and work and child's school, grade, one teacher reference, hobbies and activities outside of school, and a detailed list of any conflicts with my proposed rehearsal schedule. Then, when I cast, I require all actors to sign a *letter of commitment form,* but the young people must have a parent sign with them. I personally talk with at least one parent of every child I cast to make sure they understand the time and transportation commitment involved. My university also requires all minors have their parents sign a basic *injury waiver form* for this activity.

Depending on how many young people you plan to cast in your show, or the popularity of perhaps the one child role in your play, you may have huge numbers of young people appear. When I held auditions for *The Little Match Girl,* I put a call out for girls between the ages of *10* and *12.* I had *89* little girls show up for one role. Fortunately, I was prepared.

If you expect a large turnout, I recommend you do as I did and schedule a separate audition time for young people. If you need adults present to read or interact with the young people, pull in a few volunteers to help you. Most important, I recommend you avoid a one-at-a-time system. If your audition period is from 9:30 AM to 11:30 AM on a Saturday, announce that anyone auditioning must be present by 8:45 AM to fill out forms. This way you can create an audition experience for young people that will make them feel like they have been given something worthwhile for their effort and it will fulfill your educational responsibility to many future theatre artists and/or appreciators.

I put my *89* candidates through the following: *15* minutes of introduction and talk about my behavioral expectations, my understanding of and my approach to the play, and my high excitement about the artistic outcome; *20* minutes of fun movement exercises like *walk through worlds,* where I have my piano accompanist create mood and I ask everyone to move about in several imaginary worlds, existing underwater, walking on an earth covered with hot coals, moving gravity free, surviving on a planet full of plants and grass made of broken glass, floor to ceiling cotton candy air, knee-high mud, and so on.

As these progress, I often stop and add complexity, like working with partners, helping injured others, problem-solving like building shelters in groups of four, and so on. This work allows me to identify physical and personality types appropriate to the role(s) I am seeking to fill. This process also reveals ensemble skills and levels of risk taking, as well as imagination and physicalization skills.

Then, I spend *40* minutes assessing acting skills and vocal qualities. With my *89* little girls, I placed one of my adult actors at one end of the room and told each girl she must approach this actor and try to get him to help her with something in another part of the room. Whenever I saw a little girl that was a possible candidate for the role, I usually added some more complexity to the improvisation so I could see a little more.

One little girl asked the actor to help her mother who was having a baby somewhere on the other side of the room, so off they went. After they played that scene, I told them to play it again but this time they would be unable to find the mother at first. I was overwhelmed at the response—believable, emotionally connected tears and panic poured forth. I whispered to one of my female adults actors to lie down on the floor, and the scene found an end. I eventually cast this little girl in the lead.

At this point I announced a *10*-minute break for everyone. While the girls were getting a drink or visiting the rest room, my staff and I cut the group down to about *6* first-round finalists. When we gathered again, I told them how proud I was of them for showing me a professional attitude by working so hard. Many times it is more a matter of look, readiness, and blend than just talent. I told them to try and compete only with themselves while they are young, because unless they commit to several years of serious training when they are older, they will never really know their true talent level. Then and only then should they take competition with others seriously. It is very important that *all* young people leave feeling they have accomplished something worthwhile and have succeeded to a high degree.

I then announced the names of the *6* girls I wanted to keep a bit longer and dismissed the rest. If I needed to look for other skills like specific dancing skills, singing skills, or gymnastic skills, I would need to make time for that also, probably toward the beginning of our time together.

Next, I had the *6* girls read a couple of cold scenes from the script with my adult actor and I added minimal blocking. Then I gave them each a monologue and told them to memorize it and be ready to perform it at callbacks next Saturday at the same time. I then gave them all a copy of the script and told them to study it and bring it with them, because I would be looking for an actress who really understood her character and the play.

At the second Saturday callback, I combined my adult finalists with my girl finalists. When auditioning young people, it is very important that you see the *minimum* amount of skills and attributes you can live with during the actual audition. If you don't see it in the audition, you probably won't see it in performance, especially in young, preteen actors. I needed to have a *little match girl* who could be heard in a large space, connect with one very serious crying scene, handle some minor choreography, and perform naturally while projecting a wonderful sense of humor in the face of endless despair. Believe it or not, I had two strong candidates.

I ended up double-casting them, but I don't recommend this unless you are sure you have the time to serve them both and still attend to the rest of your cast. I do recommend *understudying* major child roles. Many young people like to do this and survive quite well even though they don't get to go on. When I say understudy, I mean someone who has the role memorized and has watched the blocking several times. Then, in an emergency, I could put that person in the show with one three-hour rehearsal the day of the show. Often times, I cast my understudy in a small role so she is in the show—I have even been known to create such a role.

Being aware of personal traits in young actors is also part of the casting process. The old stand-by terms like self-discipline, precociousness, high social skills, good behavior, and a good work ethic must not be forgotten. How a child puts this high-status experience into perspective is also very important. When I was casting *Step on a Crack* a few years back, I had two outstanding *11*-year-old finalists for the lead role of Ellie. Then, on the last day, I happened to ask them—at different times—how they thought this experience would affect them. The first girl said it was really going to be exciting as long as she could still work soccer league into the schedule. The second girl said she was excited because now she would soon become a TV star—and she was very serious. Needless to say, I cast the first girl who was able to put the whole experience into a workable perspective with other things going on in her life.

Overall, when you choose to cast young people in your show, you must commit to becoming more than just a director, you must commit to the role of mentor, teacher, and role model as well. If you have lots of young people in your cast, I recommend you appoint an acting coach to be in charge of them at all times.

Rehearsal Tips

Any good director prepares for rehearsals each day just as a good teacher spends time preparing for classes each day. The preparation time is spent on strategies that will efficiently move the cast towards opening day. Good actors know how to contribute to this process in keeping rehearsals spontaneous, thought-provoking, and creative in nature. When you add young people to this formula, you must add preparation that will accommodate their needs as well. Here are some tips as you begin preparing your rehearsals:

- Schedule young people for rehearsals only when their presence is absolutely essential.
- If you have lots of young people in your cast, someone must be responsible for them at all times. Make this person not a babysitter, but a teacher or acting coach. Use waiting time productively. If you have young people sitting around too much, you have not done a good job of preparing your rehearsal schedule.
- Bonding your intergenerational cast is critical to achieving an artistic ensemble. I recommend daily use of group warm-ups before beginning each rehearsal, warm-ups where the cast must interact. Schedule in some bonding extracurricular time also—take everyone for pizza, or a trip to visit something that will connect to the play. Birthday celebrations are great; I have been known to secretly twist an adult cast member's arm to have a birthday during the month of our rehearsals whether they actually did or not. Celebration is a great bonding tool.
- Schedule in optional time for acting work with young people (and adults). I do this in the late afternoons and hold my regular rehearsals at night.
- The most important lesson you can teach young people early in the rehearsal process is what it means to *stay in the scene,* that is, listening and reacting, playing the primary event and the given circumstances, thinking continuous questions from the character's viewpoint, moving from one appropriate task or daily agenda to another, and so on.
- Less talk and more action is a good motto to live by when working with young people; use lots of improvisation.
- Know the difference between *modeling* an idea and *demonstrating* an idea. Modeling sets helpful parameters, while demonstrating takes too much creativity away from the actor. Despite endless conversation, leading questions, and improvisation, many young people may not give you what you want and you will have to model actual vocal and physical parameters before they understand the "kind" of behavior you want. This is not the same as taking an actor's line and telling him, "Say it like this," or "Do this with your body," and then you demonstrate. However, the younger the child, the more you may have to regress to modeling and even demonstrating in some cases.
- Remember that young people run until they drop, while adults simply get tired and drag on. During a final dress rehearsal for *A Wrinkle in Time,* my 10-year-old boy lead was working really hard until we stopped momentarily to fix some lighting problems. Moments later

when I called places and action, the boy did not respond; I went up on stage to look for him and there he was, right in the middle of the stage next to a platform, sound asleep amidst the noise and chatter of the entire cast and crew. Keep this in mind when scheduling rehearsals.

- One of the real paradoxes in working with young people is trying to understand how in real, everyday life young people can be so natural and animated in voice and body, yet the minute they try to naturalize printed dialogue, they sound and look totally fake and unconnected. To naturalize young people, use improvisation to find organic and believable voice and body; make the actors aware at that moment that this is what you want, then return to the script. Remember that at this age they are *concrete thinkers*. When a child is struggling with trying to naturalize a line from the script, I often interrup and ask an unrelated question like, "Where did you say your family went on vacation this summer?" The child instantly and unconsciously answers in a connected and natural sounding voice. *"That is what I want,"* I say, "did you hear that?" Then we return to the line.

- Be aware that the communication dynamics of young people are usually different from adult communication dynamics; the younger the child, the more indirect the communication, meaning children usually carry on conversations while doing other daily agenda things like working on a puzzle or playing with toys. They seldom make eye contact, hence, the worst acting position to put a child in is standing up and talking to another actor for a long time, or standing, watching, and listening for a long time. (Professional playwrights who specialize in writing for children understand this—read Susan Zeder's *Doors*. The two lead boys play games through most of their rich dialogue. Seldom do they sit or stand statically and talk to each other.) Give them daily agenda.

- If it is essential for a child to hit an emotional moment in the play, but you simply cannot lead the child to a natural release, keep in mind, children are highly connected physical beings. Allow them to physicalize it—yes, fake it and try to get there from an outside-in approach. Because young actors are very physically connected, this may release the real thing; it may become a successful attempt at using such outside-in approaches as Michael Chekhov's "psychological gesture" or the new "Alba Emoting" system.

- Many times young people respond better to things broken down into small, compact, comprehensible units. Hence, feel free to work in detail with them on performance beats and dramatic rhythms, but be sure you know what you want, because young people will lock it in very quickly. Task mastery is their focus, not social nuance, and it is risky to start changing things at the last minute as pressure mounts.

- When rehearsal is over, make sure you or some other responsible staff person remains at rehearsal until every child has been picked up—do not let them convince you that they will be just fine.

- Require all young people to bring a pencil and notebook every day to rehearsal to write feedback notes in. Then, tell them you will talk over these notes with them just before their next rehearsal begins.

- Warning: be prepared for all actors under the age of *12* to have the entire script memorized at the first or second rehearsal. One little girl I used as the lead in an original script was the only child in a cast of 14 adults. She had her couple of hundred lines memorized by the second rehearsal—*and everyone else's lines as well.* She had the entire play memorized! (This is not uncommon in children.) The problem was that she about drove everyone else crazy because she kept giving other actors their lines whether they wanted them or not. We had a talk and all ended well—but be warned.

- Warning: all rehearsal periods are cursed with some degree of stress—be conscious of how you handle stress directed towards young people; you may do unnecessary damage to a fragile soul. Try to handle your stress with straight talk about your fears and expectations, and above all, have a sense of humor and show it.

- Run of show: thank goodness a date is usually set for opening a show, or some directors would never stop rehearsing. Other directors never really let go of a show—they keep right on giving notes until the very end. I do believe some feedback from the director is appropriate through the first couple of performances in front of an audience, especially when young people are in the cast, so continue feedback to young actors during this period.

Communicating with Young People

As I mentioned earlier, young actors see the same world we all see, they just understand it a bit differently based on what stage of development they are passing through and what life experiences they have had thus far. The most important thing I can tell you about communicating with young people is *to be yourself and respect young people as equal human beings capable of most anything.* In addition to this, it helps to know what makes a young person at a certain age tick. Consider this easy model:

Age of Child	Motivation in Life	Directing Use
Ages 4–8	"Am I a good person?"	Actors must know they are pleasing you as a person.
Ages 9–12	"Can I master the task?"	Actors must know that you are pleased with their ability to master the role.
Ages 13–15	"Who am I?"	Actors must know they successfully "fit" into the ensemble and can fulfill group expectations.

The child in the *4–8 year old category* still centers on family and close-to-home friends and environments. When you communicate with this child, remember the content and size of his/her world. When you communicate with a child actor, relate your discussion to his/her world. At this age, you are most likely to get selfish personality and cute much of the time; unfortunately, this oftentimes leads to very little play comprehension and role consistency. Staying in the scene is a real challenge at this age—nearly impossible. If the play seeks to maintain the "fourth wall," you may wish to reconsider using this age child.

The child in the *9–12 category* has a much bigger world to base communication on. His/her world now includes many more people, experiences, and interests. Rules, task completion, and social negotiation are strong concerns of this child. Most young actors in this category are highly motivated to solve any task you give them, but they still cannot think hypothetically like adults actors and are pretty limited to trial and error. Hence, you may get strong and precise physical and vocal mastery of the role, but limited emotional depth and insight.

The teen in the *13–15 category* possesses just about all the mental equipment adults have, except for the ability to successfully apply it all. Young actors at this age may suddenly exhibit great shyness and embarrassment and then moments later offer something outrageous and inappropriate.

They are hypothesis-testing and, in the early teens, they often come up with incomplete solutions.

Early teens are my favorite age to work with because they can often reach real emotional depth with freshness and insight. Despite the behavioral regression to an earlier category when threatened, the patient director who learns to "hook" talented young teens will be rewarded with creative and exciting performances.

Just remember, when talking through ideas, problems, or most anything with young people, give a little thought to how big their world is, what dominates their interest in that world, and what the major life question is for that particular age. Then, phrase your question or advice in a way that connects with what you now know about young people. I further recommend you try pulling young actors aside when you wish to communicate critically and then whisper to them so only they can hear.

Gifted and Talented Identifiers

About one decade ago, I started my Theatre School for Youth, a gifted and talented program in theatre which now has two divisions, one for preteens and one for teens. The development of both theatres arts potential and human potential was the main goal of this program from the very beginning—to create quality characters on and off the stage. I built in a healthy diet of required ensemble training, focused both on drama/theatre work and on positive everyday living—a demand to consciously improve one's physical, intellectual, and psycho-social skills.

Now my staff and I faced a critical question: *What behaviors identify an untrained young person as gifted and talented in the theatre art of acting?* We began the identification process by looking for traditional gifted and talented traits (above average intelligence, high creativity and imagination, and high task motivation), but looking exclusively within a drama/theatre context. Auditions required one prepared monologue, improvisational work with the interviewer, an interview assessing motivation, among other things, and a prepared resume and picture. Much to everyone's surprise, five categories of giftedness clearly emerged.

Consider the specific needs of your script and your overall production and then prioritize which of these gifted and talented identifiers are absolutely essential to your situation and which G & T identifiers you can let slide a little. Then, when auditioning, keep an eye open for young people having one or more of these gifted and talented identifiers, especially those that will serve your directing needs.

1. Emotional Connection.

Refers to an ability to instantly and honestly feel, share, and physicalize genuine emotions while in role. Discussion: Working improvisationally with an eleven-year-old boy, I asked him to play a tough, uncooperative youth who had just been detained by me, the policeman, for shoplifting. He was to continue this behavior as I interrogated him until he heard the word "parents." Then, the boy was to look away and visualize how hurt his parents would be when they came to get him, begin to quietly cry, and change his attitude to one of cooperation. (Create any type of image-release moment you wish that you think serves both the child and the play.) This particular boy could connect with his visual image and cry in about five seconds. Such a skill is a gift in an untrained actor, especially in an eleven-year-old boy. Maybe about one in forty possess this gift to some extent without training.

2. Interpretive Communication

Refers to an ability to create and send exceptionally clear meaning through voice and/or gesture while in role. Discussion: Sometimes actors, especially young people, struggle when attempting to naturalize lines from a script—even when they are wonderfully natural doing improvisations. A young actor possessing this gift is able to "own" his/her lines immediately. Other young actors may be held back by low reading skills or an inability to sense psycho-social context quickly. I often test and teach this skill by using a few lines of nonsense dialogue and then ask young actors to play the lines based on a given set of circumstances—then I change them.

From here I move to the actual script for a discussion of psycho-social context and some cold line readings. To free the body, which often lags behind the voice when communicating meaning in role, I have the young actors practice busy daily agenda that would fit the scene context, such as folding clothes, working on a project, or playing at something. Then, I have them add dialogue to this natural action, and watch to see if this allows the body to better connect with the voice in sending interpretive communication.

3. Physical Performance

Refers to someone who possesses a truly outstanding vocal instrument (stage voice) or an outstanding physical instrument (stage movement) while in role (and usually out of role). Discussion: Just think of the first time you heard the voice of James Earl Jones or watched Dustin Hoffman move so naturally in character. In a young untrained actor, these would be gifts. One eight-year-old girl I worked with on our main stage was blessed with outstanding diction and projection, although she struggled with interpretive communication. One ten-year-old boy auditioning for my program instantly stuck out due to his wonderful ability to move with grace, exactness, variety, and efficiency—very little waste. Such skills are gifts.

4. Natural Charisma

Refers to the ability of someone to unconsciously draw others to them, to engage their focus through organic, chemical attraction while in role. (Such a trait usually, but not always, exists out of role as well.) Discussion: For a long time, I was sure that natural charisma could be explained away through gifted physical performance, but I was wrong. Although physical gifts may be involved somehow, natural charisma truly is a category in and of itself—defying explanation at this time. Talent agents call it "edge."

5. Ensemble Commitment

Refers to the innate ability to build trust and to the desire to be a caretaker of others, through an often mysterious sense of social balance and a deep intuitive understanding of others, while in role and out—always a joy to have around. Discussion: This young actor often appears in the middle of the pack in other areas, yet the minute this person joins your cast, things seem warmer, go smoother, and everyone in the cast seems more willing to take artistic risks. This is the young actor who comes up to me after the rehearsal and tells me that he/she is worried about another member of the cast because he/she seems to be so unhappy. I did not expect such a category to emerge, but it makes sense because ensemble is at the heart of high performance in any group.

Keep in mind, most all of the young actors we used in the identification process were raw beginners or had very little acting experience; certainly none could be said to possess a high level of learned theatre technique. Even more interestingly, most students identified as gifted and talented fit two or more categories.

Of course, all of these categories are essential tools to any actor regardless of the performance space or the play. However, if you must choose between limitations, as most directors of amateur theatre must do, these gifted and talented identifiers may be helpful to you when auditioning young people between the ages of eight and fifteen. For example, if you are producing in an intimate little space, certainly emotional connection will be easily observed by all. If you are producing in a huge barn, diction and projection will be a major concern. If a child role calls for some "hot" emotional moments, emotional connection will be a priority, and so on.

Intergenerational Performance Power

The combination of adult actors creating theatre with child actors—when done well—provides directors with visual and emotional dynamics that simply cannot be duplicated by having a young adult play a child's role. The risk *is* higher, but so are the rewards when the final product is artistically excellent. The cinema has capitalized on this power for years, but only in the last couple of decades have child roles grown in number and in contextual quality at the same time; see *Stand By Me, Witness,* and *Little Man Tate*—just to mention a couple.

The work of professional playwrights like Susan Zeder has broken new ground in providing live theatre with scripts that feature quality child roles; *Step on a Crack, Doors,* and *Mother Hicks* are three outstanding examples. Personally, I have found that ensemble work is much higher when I cast intergenerationally. The logic is simple; adults tend to become mentors and role models for children and children tend to respond with accelerated maturity and self-discipline in an attempt to become more like the adults. Both children and adults tend to demonstrate a higher degree of professional behavior when working together.

Concerning Special Talents, or Whose Disability* Is It, Anyway?

How to Include and Direct People with Disabilities

by J Ranelli

"Do they eat spaghetti?" was the question as the hostess led members of the National Theatre of the Deaf into her spectacular dining room cantilevered over the edge of the Pacific Ocean. I assured her that "they" had been seen doing so on several occasions, she rolled her eyes, tapped her forehead, and blushed.

For years after, the question, "Do deaf people eat spaghetti?" was one of the catch phrases that brought humor to moments of tribulation during the company's international travels.

Dumb question? Of course not. Subtext: an apology. "I really don't know anything about deaf people. I don't sign. I'm a little nervous, I'm sorry. Do

---

*The terms "disability" and "disabled" are used here because of their familiarity rather than their accuracy. The search for a better term has given us a range of alternatives from "differently abled" to various forms of "challenged"; none of which is less likely to be used dismissively, as labels. As with all labels, it is necessary to look past the summary or the stereotype to the unique qualities of the individual.

you think it'll be all right?" Ignorant? Sure, but who isn't—didn't we have a president who believed that trees could kill?

How did the actors feel? They laughed and said that the woman had, at least, thought to offer a proper meal after the performance when most receptions consist of trays of (more costly) sweets and urns of coffee that keep you up all night. And besides, the view was terrific!

First, let's take the narrow definition of disability that most of us accept as operational within the day-to-day conduct of our lives (and a useful definition it is to anyone who does not fall within it), one that considers disability as an *impairment* of function made obvious by unmistakable outward manifestation: a wheelchair, a white-tipped cane, hearing aids, braces, and so on.

Now, let's turn this definition around some—consider the poetry and music of blind artists, the magical theatre of sign language, the graphic arts created by men and women in wheelchairs—and we find very special *abilities*. Talent.

For the most part, this talent is underused because of some of the negative connotations of the "operational" definition—most damaging, of course, is the notion that the disabled have not so many special talents as special problems. Well, the special problem may be one's own discomfort, which has been enough to create a psychological barrier that has made the disabled nearly invisible. Often we just don't see "them"!

The theatre, which is supposed to be a center of humanitarian sympathies, an artistic, caring place, is no less guilty and may be far more culpable than the rest of society; for it is our proclaimed interest in the human condition and the examination of it through rehearsal and performance that secures everything from our self-esteem to our non-profit status. Sure, we make "entertainment," but we want our customers to leave the theatre with the smiles and tears of identification, recognition—insight!

Schools of drama, especially professional programs, generally make no special effort to recruit or encourage disabled students to participate, and so there are few who grow up thinking that professional or avocational theatre is a possibility. Talent neglected.

But things are changing. There is an increased awareness due to achievement, advocacy, and legislation. And certainly there would be no reason for this appendix if there were not some talented individuals who have managed to pursue their interests, develop their skills, and so become "eligible" for inclusion in theatre productions. Most of these who have career interests have become associated with such professional groups as the National Theatre of the Deaf and Access Theatre. These and other groups are raising consciousness as they create exciting theatre and new theatre forms that are often the envy of the rest of us. In some cases they have developed rehearsal and performance techniques that have influenced drama teachers and theatre companies around the world. So, while it may be nobody's obligation to crusade for the disabled, perhaps directors and producers who read this (all of whom have shared the maddening experiences of the talent hunt that David Young describes in his section on casting) might serve themselves if they look at the wider horizon.

For anyone who chooses to do so, the rest is simple. There is really no rule or set of rules that govern a rehearsal involving disabled actors. You'll probably end up making more frequent allowance for the old familiar, the actors who always have some breathless excuse for being late or unprepared. You may want to include this sort of dysfunction in a wider definition of disability itself.

The question is one of *access* and access is mainly *courtesy*.

The creative processes do not require special conditions. All that's needed are whatever arrangements it takes to insure that everyone in the rehearsal can get to and from the workspace and participate in the interpersonal exchange of the work itself.

The details of access depend, of course, on the individual circumstances—elevators and handrails in some cases, sign language interpreters in others. What you will find is that disabled individuals will go the extra mile to fill in the gaps, to cope when arrangements are less than ideal. For background, contact groups who deal with disability and ask what to do and how to go about doing it; this is no more or no less than a director would do in any other circumstance—learning something of military customs and bearing for a production of *The Caine Mutiny Court Martial*, brushing up your Shakespeare for a production of *Kiss Me, Kate* or perhaps reading Marcel Pagnol before you begin work on *Fanny*—in order to prepare for work.

You do not have to be a medical expert, a health care authority or a physical therapist. Just make a few calls and find out what is needed to insure access and then to talk things over with your prospective actors—nothing new in that.

One question that comes up is the one of text—if the character is not written as a disabled person, isn't it unfair to the writer or confusing to the audience to add such an obvious element that has neither explanation nor justification in the text? Well, the same reservation is applied to race and ethnicity. Here are some answers: 1. Base your decision on experience, not polemic—try things, see what you discover. If you go into an audition or a rehearsal content to justify the assumptions you began with, what's the point? 2. The goal should be equal access to all parts for all actors. The one who brings the right stuff gets the part. No debate can produce the magic of transformation and empathy that we look for in the presence of a single human being on a stage. The injustice is not in casting this way or that, it is in the denial of access. 3. Access guaranteed, it's up to the director to decide if any aspect of an actor's presence is or is not appropriate for the production. There is no reason to cast a blind actor even if you are looking for a blind soldier; maybe a sighted person on crutches will play it better. 4. Directors and audiences will grow rather to accept imaginative casting for its special advantages than fear it for its challenge to literal values—if we give ourselves the opportunity. (One of the best portrayals of Hamlet in a college production was one several years ago; the Prince was played by a young woman who got the part because she dealt with the language better than anyone else in the class.)

In my experiences with disabled actors—in plays with disabled characters—I can remember only a few when the actor's disability and the character's actually "matched up"; after all we're looking for collaborators, not cups and saucers. In plays where no characters are disabled, a surprising number of audience members report "not even noticing" an actor's disability (invisible?!). Others have said that they assumed the character was written and played as presented and were surprised to learn that the actor was disabled. Of course, I've had the reverse—a disabled character played by an actor without disability—with audiences surprised to learn that the actor was *not* disabled. Only once was a casting choice criticized—a commercial producer took me to task for "adding a disability" where none was written. He was, in turn, surprised to learn that the author supported the choice. And so on. The range of response only illuminates the range of possibility. The literal or symbolic value of anything on a stage is a matter of directorial choice—frame it or blend it—a matter of craft, not policy.

Some examples: A person who appears at an audition in a wheelchair may read his or her lines without much movement—this could be due to a reluctance to call attention to the wheelchair, but we all know, from watching countless presentations by auditioners who are inexperienced or just scared out of their wits, that it could also be an "actor problem." So, just tell the candidate to "use the space"—same as always. Good for the actor and good for the director, who will get a sense of the values offered by a kind of movement not familiar to most of us. Later, if you are interested in casting a person, you can devote part of an interview session to discussion of his or her particular disability. No one will be offended; all you have to do is admit your own inexperience and ask if there is anything you need to know about the person's routine that might help. The actor in the wheelchair may tell you that he or she needs to have a few seconds every hour for muscle stretching or that, even though your building has ramps and elevators, the hill from the parking lot is too steep for an easy climb (it happens!) and it may take a stage manager a few seconds to help out. If you don't have ramps, check around—there are temporary and portable versions available. If you prepare up front, it usually doesn't get any more "difficult" than that.

You may find that a deaf person is interested in one of your productions, or you may find that you are interested in the theatrical element a deaf actor can bring to a given part. (See what Peter Sellars achieved by casting Howie Seago in his production of *Ajax* at the Kennedy Center.) What you will discover is that the deaf person already has the communication skills required to get along even with those who know no sign language. However, if you know that deaf persons are interested in auditioning or if you are seeking them out, it is an elementary courtesy of have an interpreter present; the actor is entitled to have access to everything within earshot, and an interpreter's job is to guarantee that. (But be careful about the assistant stage manager who "learned a little finger spelling at camp in seventh grade." If budget is a problem, talk it over with your candidate; he or she may have access to institutional funding for interpreters.) Once rehearsals begin, you will find that communication will develop rapidly, thanks to the special skills of the "disabled" person. By the way, once you move away from the table or intimate room, you may also find that a flashing light is a more effective way of stopping a scene for a note than shouting or waving your arms. Again, not an extreme adjustment. But what about musicals? Well, songs can be signed and there are deaf dance companies!

For a blind actor, the same. Ask questions and just use your head. Have the stage manager "spike" rehearsal-room furniture that is not part of the ground plan so that tables and chairs can be kept or returned to consistent places during work (no problem if the director wants to move his or her chair around—it's the empty chairs that can't put out a hand). A little advance planning can also reduce any problems that may be associated with dressing and makeup. Again, confer with the actor and all the problems will go away—especially the most serious, one's own insecurity.

If the actor also happens to be a child, do the same as you would with any child; talk to the parents.

Information you gain from conferences, research and advance planning should be communicated to the producer and the stage managers so that everyone is informed.

Now that you have made your casting choice and been considerate of special needs, be a little selfish. Look closely at the actors and learn something about special talents. Beware stereotypes here as in all situations: not all blind actors are serene (!) but there may be a keenness to their listening that is tangible just as there is a heightened physical presence when an actor's language engages the entire body as American Sign Language does.

So, to sum up, if you spot a talent, talk with the actor, contact agencies and organizations who can give you specific information beyond the scope of these notes, and go to work! That's all. Again, the biggest problem will be your own insecurity, and that will pass quickly.

And, for your opening night party, try spaghetti.

Here are some references:
1. Very Special Arts is an organization dedicated to the creative efforts of the disabled in the same way that Special Olympics is concerned with athletic effort. Write to Very Special Arts, 1331 F St., N.W., Washington, DC 20004. Every state has a chapter of Very Special Arts, and the National Office will give you that contact.
2. Actor's Equity, the professional actors' union, has a committee on Performers with Disabilities (PWD), which can be very informative. In addition to maintaining a directory of performers, the committee can offer advice to professional and amateur producers. Write to the committee c/o Actors Equity, 165 W. 46th St., New York, NY 10036.
3. The National Information Center on Deafness, Gallaudet University, Washington, D.C. 20002. (202) 651-5052 (voice or TTD).
4. The Lighthouse, which has a long history of theatre with blind actors in addition to its more general services, 111 E. 59th St., New York, NY 10022.
5. For others look in the Yellow Pages: if there are no specific listings, look under "Associations."

How to Stage Musical Numbers

Dr. Nancy Vunovich

Staging the musical number is a wonderful opportunity for the director to use his or her imagination to the fullest. But in order to bring the imagination into play, a director must insure certain things prior to the actual staging.

To begin with, the director must examine the score or listen to the music of the number carefully. One hopes a director does not undertake the job of doing a musical unless he or she can read music, but too often a director may not have sufficient musical knowledge to competently read a score. If that is the case, it might be advantageous to have the musical director or accompanist play the score a number of times for the director varying the tempo and the interpretation of the music. By doing this, a director can hear when a particular sound will further the concept of the musical. And, if the director is examining the lyrics of the song at the same time, he can decide whether he would prefer the music to become slower or faster at certain points in order to emphasize important words or phrases that point out plot or character definition that he wants to make with the song. And the director can discuss with the music director how to make these points and still be compatible with the music director's interpretation of the score.

Equally important is consultation with the choreographer. Some songs demand a great deal of choreography, some songs require a little, and some none. When choreography is required, it is very important that the director has conveyed his concept and interpretation of a particular song to the choreographer; this way, time is not wasted with altering the dance after performers have spent their time learning a routine that must be discarded or altered because it does not fit.

Working with the designers to discover what the set will look like, what set pieces or props will be available, whether costumes will help or hinder the staging,and what the lighting designer has in mind will help the director in determining the staging and will save what might become future headaches in the total creative process.

At this point, let me urge that the director not rely too heavily on what he has seen or heard previously. Too often directors recall a Broadway production and want to mimic that staging when it simply is not physically possible for either designers or performers to repeat it. And how much more enjoyable for an audience to see a totally new staging of a song rather than a pale imitation of someone else's work. We all know that more than one singer can perform a song and make it memorable. The same certainly holds true for the director of a musical and those elements he incorporates into a number.

For example, recently I directed a production of *Pajama Game,* a musical comedy set in a garment factory and concerning a feud between labor and management. The show, originally produced on Broadway in the early 1950s, used the characters of Babe, a factory worker, and Sid, a new management employee, to emphasize the differences of the workers in the factory, but, nevertheless, fall in love.

After declaring their love for the first time in the ballad, "Small Talk," Sid and Babe almost immediately reiterate their love in a lighter way with the song "There Once Was a Man," this song having a definite hillbilly sound that was popular during that particular time. The first chorus, sung by Sid, refers to men who slew dragons, gave away kingdoms, and ate apples, but ends by stating that he (Sid) loves Babe more than any of these men. In the next chorus Babe sings that women have swum the channel, taken poison, and caused the Trojan War for the men they love, but she loves Sid back more than any of these. On the final chorus they duet, stating they love each other "more than a hangman loves his rope, more than a dope fiend loves his dope, more than an Injun loves his scalps, more than a yodeler loves his Alps," etc. ending with "I love you more."

The script indicates that the song was originally performed at a railway in the factory (most likely a drop depicting a railway); the film moved the number to a convertible. However, since my stage was limited in terms of space and number of sets possible, I consulted with the designer to see if the number could not be performed in the already established sewing machine factory. No problem! Then I wanted to make sure there was a sewing machine table sturdy enough for the two performers to stand on and with enough room between the actual machines for them to move. With the music director I agreed that a more rollicking tempo (the kind of bass rhythm that one shouts "Hiyo Silver" to) would aid the make-believe adventurousness of the lyrics, and, rather than the hillbilly vocal line, would better serve the childish boastings of the two newly enamored individuals. Thus the work chairs, with Babe stretched across them, became the English Channel, the screw driver which Sid was using to fix a machine became the sword with which he slew the dragon and the scepter that he gave away, a piece of pajama material became his cape for his swashbuckling derring-do, the table became the Alps that they scaled together. And, in the final moment of the song, Sid jumped from the table, then Babe leaped into his arms and he carried her off.

In fact, the song almost staged itself—but it would not have if the design and musical elements had not been discussed ahead of time.

Once the early work with designers, musicians, and choreographers is accomplished, it is time to begin working with the actors on the staging of musical numbers. Assuming that earlier work has been done on developing characterization by the director with the actors, the songs in a musical should be a natural outgrowth of environment and situation. The unnatural element is, of course, that dialogue and thoughts are suddenly being sung rather than spoken. In recent musicals librettists and composers have become much more adept at merging action and dialogue into the script and music. But earlier musicals still need some assistance from the director. Sometimes scripts have to be studied thoroughly by a director to provide motivations for songs. In *Pajama Game,* a line of Sid's, saying he needs five more minutes to *fix something* before he and Babe leave on a date puts the screwdriver in his hand and moves them to the sewing machine table.

Actors themselves can be very helpful in finding ways to develop staging. I always insist that actors be extremely familiar with their music and lyrics before I stage a number so that they can concentrate on the blocking without the obstacle of searching for notes or words at the same time. That way they can use props or relate to the other actors without the problem of script and/or score in their hands. Gestures flow more easily and earlier in the rehearsal process. Without the script in his hand, the actor who played Sid picked up the screwdriver he had used in "There Once Was a Man" at the climactic moment (at the end of Act I) when he has fired Babe and perhaps ruined their romance. Alone on stage, he slammed the screwdriver into his palm as he reprised, in a bitter manner, a portion of an earlier ballad—"better forget her," then threw the tool on the sewing machine and exited, showing his frustration and heartbreak. We kept the bit!

The screwdriver business worked so well that, at the end of the show when Sid has managed to foil a strike and save the company, Babe offers him the screwdriver just as a narrator says, "I told you this play was full of symbolism." This is enough motivation for Sid and Babe to begin the final reprise of "There Once Was a Man."

Solos, duets, or even trios are easier for the director to stage if he examines the script, the lyrics, works with his production team as well as the actors toward imaginatively creating staging that will further the concept of the play and be pleasing and original to the audience.

Working with large numbers of people, however, demands more of the director. Once again, most staging with groups should appear natural rather than regimented, unless one is doing a Gilbert and Sullivan operetta where a 19th-century style of performance still seems to prevail. I have found that if a director does the same kind of character investigation with each member of the chorus that he does with major actors, it pays off. If each person, for example, who forms the chorus of River Citians in *The Music Man* becomes a member of a family, determines his or her occupation, background, and mood, his or her actions and reactions will vary in a group song. Then all the director has to do is select and point up those actions at appropriate times in the song.

If the director wants the chorus action to appear more choreographed, he can take a different tack. Again using *Pajama Game* as an example, the song "Racing with the Clock" introduces the audience to the factory workers and their work. Improvising initially with the actors, I asked them to indicate their work pattern at the sewing machines as well as their physical feelings (tiredness, energy, etc.), layer on their mood (hung over, flirtatious, irritated, etc.), then physicalize these things in a pattern of movement. Selecting certain movements after a time, then varying the movements with individual chorus members, made an interesting pattern for the audience to follow. Thus, while one worker stretched, a second touched her aching back, a third sewed at her machine, and a fourth dropped a finished garment into a laundry cart. On the next appropriate change in music the first held her aching back, the second sewed, etc. In other words, there was a choreographic "feel" to the action without it actually being dance—or being boring because everyone was doing the same thing at the same time. It also saved staging time when it came to a workers' slowdown later on in the show, because the workers could repeat the movements but simply perform them at a slower pace.

Allowing actors to work up full backgrounds and movement patterns on their own gives them an elevated sense of their importance to the production. It then becomes a matter of the director picking and choosing what movement from the chorus most helps convey meaning to the audience.

During the last weeks of rehearsal it becomes very important that the director allow time for the cast to settle into the staging, become comfortable with it, and realize how the director is trying to point up certain elements of the plot without taking away anyone's creativity and importance.

And, of course, during the final rehearsals it is important for the director to feel sure that the cast has settled into their performance so that the director can return to design and musical elements that can again enhance the production. Here, more than at any other time, a director can insure that the audience is going to see the best of his production. If the designers and musicians have attended earlier rehearsals, as well as production meetings on a regular basis, they probably will have anticipated the director's requests to focus lighting on a strong part of the staging while minimizing a weakness or to move an actor into a strong stage position. These are things that will enhance the drama or comedy of a moment in the script.

Although staging a musical takes a lot of preplanning on the part of the director, that individual must always be aware that there has to be change in order to achieve the best possible production.

IV

The Choreographer/Director

Professor James M. Miller

Choosing the Musical

Choosing the musical to produce in any given set of circumstances is, for me, of primary importance. I am not a director who reads a play, becomes inspired, and announces it for the next season regardless of other given conditions. Musicals are what the actors, guided by the director, designers and musical directors, make them. Evolving a concept for a production without a thought to who may be acting in it is wasted time on the amateur level. In the academic theatre, young talent with a great deal of energy and ambition but not a lot of finesse or maturity makes up the majority of available actors. These circumstances, under which I direct half the time at the University of Missouri, are not restrictions so much as challenges. The casting situation changes in our Summer Repertory Theatre. We usually have a greater age range to choose from—faculty actors and actors brought in from the outside—and I still choose a show tailored to our needs. At Tulane Summer Lyric Theatre, the producers choose the season and hire me to direct and cast a particular show using professional actors from New Orleans, New York, Los Angeles and other major cities, augmented by student or amateur ensembles.

As an acting and stage movement instructor, I am aware of students coming up through the ranks of the theatre department. I keep an eye on their developing technique, creative growth, and willingness to work with peers. This awareness of students' progress is the impetus for the musicals

Scene from *Assassins,* performed at the University of Missouri, 1992. Directed by James M. Miller.

selected to fit into our academic season. I try to choose shows that the students are capable of doing well—shows that are a challenge but with a certain accessibility. Choosing musicals that have characters with realistic age ranges for the students of ages 18 to 24 is one way to boost the chances for success. Musicals that the students are capable of singing and dancing in some creditable manner are chosen. And selecting a musical that can be built with the scenic and costume budget allotted is smart thinking. Although every show can be simplified, some shows demand certain expensive design elements. *My Fair Lady* needs excellent, elegant costumes because they are so integral to the plot movement of the play. *Follies* should have a knockout set and costumes for the same reason. These two shows I would not consider doing with college students because they should be played by people of the right age. Community theatres with adequate budgets and some sophisticated acting and design talent would certainly have people in the age range for these shows.

This does not mean that college students are not capable of handling all age requirements, but the show itself must be very theatrical or presentational in nature. *George M!* works for college students because of its episodic, "we are actors, telling a story" nature. We watch the young actor telling us he is going to act the part of the brash young Cohan then slowly age as his life is portrayed in song, dance, and music. In *My Fair Lady,* the audience has to immediately accept the leading actor as Shaw's Henry Higgins. The careful selection of plays can often determine the success of a production from the outset.

A second major consideration for a director is the kind of talent at his disposal. Here at Missouri, there is no dance major within the theatre department and no conservatory of music. The basic training required of "real dancers" and super singers is not our department's strong point. The musicals selected must be theatrical and the acting or performing of them must be the element stressed. I would never attempt *West Side Story* because the dancing must be outstanding, and our department cannot supply what the play demands in those terms. The same goes for *A Chorus Line.* This show is being done all over the country because of its title and box office value, with little regard for its chances of being artistically successful or even mildly believable.

The Robber Bridegroom, not a household musical title, but a show that is within the realm of most junior and high school, college and community theatres, is adaptable to each group performing it. It can be stylized in many different ways. Without being particularly dance oriented, this show lends itself to all kinds of musical movement without the requirement of years of ballet training. The songs are tricky but not out of the range of young voices, and the show depends on the chorus or ensemble for much of its flavor. The chorus creates the background and transitional elements, and the costumes and sets adapt to suit any budget. Of all the shows I've directed here at Missouri, this is the one which people seem to remember and comment on most.

Another example of suiting the show to the pool of actors at hand is our recent production of *Very Good Eddie.* I remembered the 1976 Goodspeed Opera production of this 1915 Jerome Kern musical running in New York when I lived there. Although I didn't see the show, I knew the casting requirements called for a very tall actor and actress and a very tiny actor and actress. I had four seniors who fit these descriptions. I sent away for the cast album, was not thrilled with the music at first, but thought the book had all the elements of classic farce and was suited to the kind of students who were then in the forefront of our music and theatre departments. (Three of the leads were music majors, three were theatre majors.) There were nine principal roles and a singing, dancing, and acting chorus of eight men, eight women. I had never directed anything so close to operetta and hadn't designed costumes for this period, so the show presented me with new challenges. *Very Good Eddie* is fresh and innocent and was the perfect show to follow our summer production of *Chicago,* which is full of sex, cynicism, and crime. [All the right reasons to select a show.]

Let me clear up the idea of precasting. Even though I select shows knowing there are certain students capable of playing certain roles, this fact is never announced. This saves me from excluding the brilliant young actor or actress who might show up and be better than my original casting choice. Also, I try to project casting at least two actors deep just in case the number one choice decides he doesn't want to audition.

Audience preference does not really affect my play choices. In Columbia, Missouri, our audience is made up mostly of university-related people who tend toward liberal, rather advanced artistic ideas. Our department is not censored (not that we have any desire to present *Oh, Calcutta!*) or in any way restricted by play choice. Directing a variety of styles and periods and alternating new musicals with classic ones creates a sense of proportion and balance and keeps the director from pulling the same old tricks.

One last thought about casting—a director cannot make an actor acceptable in a part he is not ready or right for. Although *Man of La Mancha* is a good show and good box office, a nineteen-year-old boy will gain nothing from playing Don Quixote if he is miscast. Sometimes directors must protect actors from themselves. An actor "stretches" only to a certain point and then becomes self-indulgent and bad for company morale as well as audience support.

Preparation

The rehearsal schedule is one of the director's safeguards against wasted time and effort. In the initial planning for the schedule, I always start at the end of the rehearsal period and plan a certain number of run-throughs. This enables the actor to find the amount of energy an entire run-through requires and how he/she is going to allot that energy over the two or more hours of the playing time. Even if this means simplifying some production numbers or elaborate material previously planned, the actors must have those run-throughs.

I generally allot a whole rehearsal for the staging of a production number with musical movement (singing with movement) and two rehearsals (6 hours) for a production number with a big dance section. Also, I plan my rehearsals by allowing time to drop back and pick up material that was learned the previous night before continuing to the next new staging. This keeps the actors from forgetting material they have already learned.

Although blocking a musical usually takes longer than blocking a straight play, there is a momentum built up from learning, dropping back, learning something new, dropping back, learning something new, etc. The actors never grow unfamiliar with material from the first rehearsals. I probably don't allow as much time for music rehearsals the first few days as most musical directors would like. But actors seem to be able to learn the music by rote as they learn the blocking and choreography. There should be several pickup rehearsals for music as the show is progressing.

Research: Costume Design

Possibly my strongest point as a director has nothing to do with directing. I design the costumes for my shows. With the design process, I get a built-in research/think period that forces me to focus on an upcoming production. The act of drawing a costume rendering is creating character—giving physical form to thoughts and images that have come to me while studying a play or its music. The costume plate also forms a directorial bond with the actor because the designer is drawing a portrait of an actor as a character. As soon as my costume sketches go up on the bulletin board in the costume shop, the actors in the production are there scrutinizing the rendering for information about their roles. The costume rendering at its best gives an idea of period, style, movement and degree of realism.

Another organizational tool of costume design that I use for preparing to direct is the costume breakdown or list. This includes breaking the play down into a costume chart by dividing the play into scenes (either the ones already noted in the script or scenes that I devise myself) and noting which characters are on stage at any given point and what they are wearing. What a character is wearing in some cases dictates what he or she can do in terms of movement and character motivation. The more ways you can take a script apart—from the standpoint of costume, dance, music scenery, and action—the more you understand it. It's like taking something mechanical apart and putting it back together—you understand the way it was made and how it functions.

Research: Music, Dance, Libretto

In researching the background of a particular musical comedy or play, it is not necessary to compose a thesis. By research, I mean a little boning up on where the play came from or what period styles the music has been based

Cabaret, performed at the University of Missouri-Columbia. Directed and choreographed by James M. Miller.

on. Just knowing a few basic facts about the original creation of the work could color your whole perception of the direction you give. If directing a production of *Funny Girl*, read a biography of Fanny Brice rather than maintaining the vision of Barbra Streisand in the part. Listen to the music of the period, find out what songs Miss Brice introduced, whom she knew and worked with in the theatre. Have all this knowledge at your disposal as you guide an actress through a portrayal of a real person who lived rather than of a mythic figure that another actress created. This research will broaden your creative perspective and help you avoid directorial clichés.

If you plan a production of *Cabaret* without reading the play on which it is based (*I Am a Camera*) or the *Berlin Stories* by Christopher Isherwood on which *I Am a Camera* was based, you will not get full value from your production. In order to understand the music and the orchestrations you must have some knowledge of the popular music and orchestrations of the late Twenties. Jazz and jazz dancing were spreading through Europe and influencing everything from art to architecture to clothing. Knowing these things makes a difference in what you say to a designer, actor, or costumer.

Years ago I directed a college production of *Dames at Sea*. The students (in the 1970s) really had no concept of the early Thirties, of the impact of the first talking movies, or of Busby Berkeley's contribution to film dance technique. I rented the movie *42nd Street* (which is really a drama with music rather than a musical comedy) in which the leading characters (later spoofed in *Dames at Sea*) believed every word they were saying. This opened the students' eyes and they were able to play these characters with some kind of emotional depth rather than a campy superficiality. This research made the comedy more accessible. Watching the movie also gave the students ideas for movement, makeup and costumes.

Any research read, seen, or heard will be invaluable in the final outcome of the production. Find out what effect the original production had on the critics and audiences of the time. The values that were new and shocking then may be old hat now, and you may have to stress different ideas in your production.

Directing the Show

In order to direct a musical, it helps if you can read music, but you don't have to be a trained musician. However, you must be musical. Some of the greatest performances in the musical theatre have come not from musicians or singers, but from actors who were musical. Rex Harrison in *My Fair Lady* comes immediately to mind, but Zero Mostel in *Fiddler on the Roof* or *A Funny Thing Happened on the Way to the Forum* or Carol Channing in *Hello Dolly* are other examples of strong musicality without great singing voices. By musical, I mean an innate response to music which we all have to some degree but of which musical performers and directors must have a bit more than most. They must be able to physicalize and vocalize this response. Fred

Astaire walking or Katharine Hepburn running across a room in her early films pictorialize musicality. This inner sense is necessary to a straight play but is more evident in a musical.

When I examine a musical play for production, it must not only have the music that the composer has written, but must also have a continuing musicality or the capacity to gain it either through direction or choreography or design elements. I explain to my students that they must feel an underscoring of the scenes between the musical numbers. They must subconsciously project that underlying musicality or pulse through the dialogue into the musical numbers. This dispels the jarring break that happens to some performers or performances when the dialogue ends and the singing begins. These transitions are successful only when the actor is carrying the musicality of the whole piece with him between planned musical interludes.

Sometimes the director has to create this underlying musicality through staging, and sometimes the dialogue itself has the rhythm/musicality already implanted. The script of *My Fair Lady* is based on Shaw's *Pygmalion*. Shaw's dialogue is the impetus for Lerner and Loewe's music and lyrics and, therefore, the adaptation from play to musical is seamless and contains its own musicality. With *Pippin*, director Bob Fosse took a mediocre libretto and turned it into a musical entity with staging and choreography.

This musicality is basic to my method of directing a musical. The show must be all of a piece. Even leading roles must be a part of the whole picture, and, in some musicals, achieving the balance is virtually impossible.

Let me try to explain how a musical number or a section of staging/choreography happens for me. First of all, I am not a trained dancer. I took classes in modern dance and ballet in college and even took classes in ballet in New York when I lived there. Although I have a rudimentary knowledge of dance, I do not know the language of dance. I cannot communicate with dancers in their own language. A combination of steps to me is not something that has come from years of arranging and rearranging steps in a classroom setting. Yet I seem to be able to direct dancers to dance certain passages with a sense of acting they have never used before. The blessing in my work is that I don't have any preconceived notion about what musical comedy "dance" is supposed to be. I don't know that the singers are supposed to sing and get off and let the dancers take over. Besides, there are not many musicals structured that way anymore.

Musical comedy movement and dance should accompany and reinforce whatever the scene or musical number is communicating. For example, the "Family Fugue" in *Stop the World, I Want to Get Off* is a musical number that exists for several reasons. For one thing, it follows a slow sentimental song

Dames at Sea,
**performed at the
University of
Missouri-
Columbia.
Directed and
choreographed by
James M. Miller.**

that tells us how much Littlechap wants a son. He has two daughters, and when his son is born and dies (following the song "Meilinki Meilchick"), his character must go on living—with a wife and two daughters and the dreary propriety he must face in his climb up the corporate ladder and through the British class system. The movement and choreography that evolved came from a note I made to myself in the margin of the script when I was first reading it—"minuet." This became the symbol for the sense of order overlaying a British household in tumult. We see the family having breakfast as they do every morning, with the underlying strains of tension showing up as Evie pours coffee into Littlechap's lap after he reminds her he has no sons. This is all mimed and choreographed. As the number progresses, the chorus of men and women become "Littlechaps" and "Evies" having the same domestic crisis all over London. The number then works itself into the "Nag, Nag, Nag" phase, and the arguments and movements become larger and take over the stage. The lost decorum is fought for by Littlechap as he sings, "My wife's voice is a symphony," but at the last minute he starts on her again with, "and I hate every bloody note." At this point all the men sing the "My wife's voice is a symphony" passage as they perform a quasi-ballet/minuet with their wives. It's a comic number that serves the structure of the plot and is entertaining at the same time. The number also breaks the sadness of the previous song "Meilinki Meilchick" and of the son's death, so that the story can pick up and take off again.

The minuet serves as a metaphor for the formal ritual of getting married, staying married, even marital sparring and marital pain. There are several reasons this choreography can happen. In the original production there was no male chorus, just Littlechap and women. In rethinking the production for our Summer Repertory Theatre, we wanted the company members to appear in at least two shows. So the chorus of the musical had to incorporate men. This gave the young actor playing the leading role some male reinforcement and liberated the choreography, in that the men in the ensemble could give sympathetic support to Littlechap's position as Everyman or comment on or oppose his actions as the play progressed.

These extra men in the show gave a new dimension to Littlechap's "I've Been Lumbered" number after he's been forced to marry Evie because of her pregnancy. The other men in the ensemble empathize with Littlechap or make fun of his predicament and keep the number from being just one more solo for the leading character. Adding their voices to some of the solo songs also gave the actor playing the leading role a chance to pull back and pace the use of his voice.

Words are, for me, another source of choreography. I don't just mean the literal meaning with accompanying motions. On the page the words have a form in their poetic arrangement that can be used to design a number or musical sequence. As written in the musical score, the words seem to lose this form or shape, but this very shape of the printed words in the libretto can be used as an organizational tool. It can be used to form a beginning, middle,and end to a sequence. A musical number can be planned according to the arrangement of the words on the page—verse, chorus, verse, chorus, dialogue, verse, chorus. Each repetition of an element can build toward the climax. If this sounds like designing production numbers by mathematical principles, the response to the music and the musical arrangement itself will thwart and facilitate any mechanical repetition that becomes clumsy or too contrived.

Choreography and movement can be used in a very subtle way to overcome vocal problems or vocal fear. I've noticed in many rehearsal periods that if an actor has to stand in one place and sing, the singing becomes the focus of what the actor, not the character, is doing. The actor will choke and become unable to control his voice. But as the character takes over and has a motivation and a reason for singing or is given an action to do, the vocal problems disappear. The actor is functioning as a character with planned choreography that reinforces the character's action objectives. This of course only goes so far. If the actor does not have it in him to hit the high F, no amount of blocking will provide him with it.

Most singers can move and sing with no disturbance of their vocal power and breathing as long as most of the movement happens from the waist down. Sustained movement with the arms above the diaphragm interferes with proper breathing for the singer and should be avoided.

Sometimes simple choreography communicates more and is more appropriate to a song or character than a complicated ballet. The actor should have plenty of time to learn whatever is expected of him, and it should suit his talents, not the director/choreographer's.

When working with non-dancers, I don't choreograph for myself and then try to teach them an elaborate combination of steps that have nothing to do with their movement strengths. I work with the actor, find out how he moves, what looks good on him right there in the rehearsal. The original choreographic idea may remain the same, but its form changes to suit the individual. There is nothing more embarrassing and uncomfortable for an audience than an actor trying to do something that is out of his range. But an audience will buy anything the actor is doing as long as it fits his strengths, looks easy and accomplished, and is musical.

Performers who are not trained dancers seem to be able to pick up movements that they watch evolve in rehearsal. Being able to choreograph for the performers on the spot—line by line—musical phrase by musical phrase—gives them an insight into the reason for the movement and its place in the dramatic structure. It is their choreography—made from them, on their bodies—and it becomes a part of their performance.

Although warm-ups would seem to be self-explanatory, I have found as a director that the side effects of pre-rehearsal exercise are more important than the more obvious initial reason for doing them. A musical is very abstract—actors come to rehearsal from the outside real world, and they cannot go right into the world of the rehearsal and the play without some transition period. Warm-ups, simple bending and stretching exercises, provide a few minutes for the actors' minds and bodies to become attuned to what is about to happen. They are preparing to work and to dream—to enter the world of the musical. I lead the warmups, and this allows them the chance to accept me as the leader—a director who is going to demand their deepest attention and concentration for the next three hours. This is not essential just for the performers, it is essential for me.

Blocking and choreography rehearsals are periods that begin with the sketching of a musical number or a section of a show. By sketching I mean laying in preliminary blocking that will change and evolve as the rest of the show takes shape. I divide the play into a series of scenes that may contain more than one musical number. Some musical numbers such as romantic ballads that are solos or duets may require less time to block than a full-cast production number. (This will sometimes surprise me and be just the opposite.) I start sketching with the bodies of the actors in front of me, then I gradually add personal details for individual characters.

Actors have good instincts and the director should be aware of what the actors are sensing in the music. Do their bodies respond a certain way? Is the music something they relate to from their own experiences? When I directed *Grease,* I found the students had an intense response to it, because they were familiar with the music and John Travolta's performance in the movie version. Also, some of their parents were teenagers in the 1950s and the students were familiar with the period through them. *Very Good Eddie,* on the other hand, set in 1915, is a period that might as well have been the Renaissance. Their response to the music was not immediate, and they only trusted what they were doing gradually. As we discussed the era, worked on motivations for dramatic action and comic bits, the music and choreography became more than just quaint. Rehearsal skirts and costumes were the final touch in helping them to understand the characters and their period.

One of the keys to a successful musical production is, unfortunately, one of the most boring things for the director/choreographer. There is no substitution for laborious drilling and polishing of musical numbers and scenes. Some directors have a knack for this—for others it is pure labor. I don't think it's something a director of amateurs can leave to an assistant either. Precision and the performers' complete comprehension of when and how to do their tasks liberates actors rather than restricts them. This is why I try to get my shows frozen as quickly as possible. The actors must have time to make their actions, reactions, movements, and motivations as instinctual as possible. In the drill and polish phase, the director should be patient and persistent. This phase of a musical takes time and effort and should not be neglected.

The magic of a musical happens when all the elements of theatre come together and no effort shows. Songs and dances should look like they are happening for the first time and are the natural progression for the characters to make. This only happens when the performers are so familiar with the material that it is second nature. Since musicals are chiefly presentational anyway, the actor must take the next step and somehow convince the audience he is having the most wonderful time in the world. The actor in a musical, or at least parts of a musical, must let the audience share his performance.

The director-actor relationship is one that changes each time I direct a show and encounter a different group of actors. I once directed a production of *Cabaret* in which I had to block every single movement for the actor playing the M.C. He was very insecure and wanted and expected me to give him the character bit by bit. As I was also choreographing the show, the actor expected the same detailed input as a director. This is not the way I like to work, but sometimes it is necessary. The actor was fine in the role once all the minute points of movement and interpretation were given him, and it was worth the effort. Other actors react to an abstract, suggestive direction that leads them to their own individual characterizations blending with the rest of the show. Actors who are dancers sometimes like to have a hand in their choreography; other dancers just want to be shown the combinations, and after they have the mechanics down, they come up with a psychological or artistic way to fit what they're doing into the rest of the production. I wish that I could say I've never given an actor a line reading, but I have. Most of these line readings are suggestive, anyway, and the actor takes it, uses it, molds it to something that works for him, or discards it as rehearsals progress and comes up with something different and better.

I always make a special point of including ensemble members (or chorus, a word which I don't use in rehearsal or programs) in the motivating analysis of the play. They need more than just directions. They need to understand that the smallest gesture or loss of concentration is felt, if not seen, by the audience. I try to make them understand that the ensemble singing, dancing, and acting is equal to one huge leading role, and that without them the show is nothing. They have to know this in order to feel they are not just moving scenery or colorful background. Actors who will not work in the ensemble are seldom recast in a leading role.

Actors in a rehearsal never seem to perform to their fullest potential unless I am invigorated and watching with as much energy as they are working. It takes so much strength to direct a musical and even more to perform one. I have never found rehearsing fun, and I don't expect the actors to just have fun either. Rehearsals are invigorating and absorbing and interesting. If someone didn't remind me, I wouldn't remember to give actors breaks. If a rehearsal is going well, they usually don't remember breaks either.

Finally, there comes a point in the precision world of the musical when the director has to give the show to the performers and realize that he (like it or not) has become superfluous. The actors must face the audience together, but the director is really not included. Since realizing this, I have enjoyed watching my shows for the first time. I used to become extremely nervous watching my work, but now I realize that it is the actors' work, in the final analysis, that is seen and heard and felt. And that's the way it should be.

V

Computers for the Musical Theatre

Easy Ways to Transpose and Make Sophisticated Recordings (Tape and Disk) for Learning, Rehearsal and Performance

Dr. Roger Gross, University of Arkansas

This is a good time for producers and directors of musical theatre. Several of the most frustrating old problems now can be brushed aside. New possibilities for efficient rehearsal are available. New ways to enrich lower-budget productions have opened up. All of this can be achieved at modest cost because of recent developments in computer technology.

These blessings spring from the integration of computers with music synthesizers and ingenious software programs for music sequencing, notation, harmonization, accompaniment, scanning . . . even composition. This union holds tremendous promise for musical theatre, and you don't have to be a computer buff or invest heavily in training to get the benefits. Even the hardware and software are inexpensive considering the wonders they perform.

This integration is made possible by the electronic music industry's shrewd decision to adopt "MIDI," a common standard for communication among instruments. MIDI is the acronym for Musical Instrument Digital Interface. Because of MIDI, almost any electronic instrument can "talk to" any other and to any computer that is equipped with the hardware/software combination called a "MIDI interface." Your keyboard or guitar can now talk to your computer; the computer can do wonderful things with these messages and pass them on to synthesizers, tape or disc recording machines, or other computers.

This will be a "wish list" of computer/music possibilities, not a "how to" manual. I will describe briefly the basic kinds of software and then suggest a number of ways you might benefit from their potential. Finally, I'll tell you how to get more information.

Music Software

Nowhere is the American dream of free enterprise better realized than in the computer software business. It is one of the last outposts where genius and effort, without major capitalization, can produce enormous achievement and economic success. Creativity and know-how are the heart of it; hardware is a relatively trivial factor. The result is an industry that is exploding with creativity. Constant, rapid change is the norm. A few years ago, none of the software I'll describe here was available. In another year, the things I describe will have been supplanted by faster, cheaper, easier programs that will do things we can only dream of today.

Sequencing

The most fundamental program is the sequencer. The name comes from the function: MIDI sequence recorder. A sequencer records musical data (not sounds) and stores it for editing and playback. Some electronic keyboards have simple on-board sequencers. Some sequencers are stand-alone "black boxes" whose only function is to sequence. The most sophisticated sequencers are computer software programs.

Think of your sequencer as the world's greatest music recorder. Greatest because of its tremendous capacity, almost limitless editing options, ease of use, and low cost. Any MIDI-equipped electronic device can input information to a sequencing program. Including your computer keyboard. You could "play" an entire symphony into your sequencer from your electronic keyboard. You can do it as one great "live" performance or one musical line at a time or one chorus, one phrase, one bar, even one role at a time. You don't have to be an accomplished performer to put your music in the sequencer. You only have to know what notes you want.

Making a Song File

Whatever your basic musical unit may be (a musical idea, a theme, a song, background score, sonata, etc.), to the sequencer it is a "song file."

Everything starts with the recording of your song file in a sequencer. Then the fun begins. Most sequencers offer three methods of input: real-time, step-time from an electronic keyboard, and step-time from a computer keyboard. The most sophisticated sequencers offer up to seven options.

Real-Time Recording

You may simply play your music into the sequencer. You can play at any tempo you like because the editing will allow you to modify the tempo later in any way you like; faster, slower, accelerando, ritardando, sustains, rubato, anything. Once the notes are recorded, they can be molded almost as freely and easily as you once molded Play-Doh.

You may play everything you have at once or one line (voice, instrument, section) at a time, overdubbing, in effect, until you have accumulated just what you want. Two of the best programs, *Performer* and *Vision* offer "tap tempo," a feature that allows you to vary the speed of your input without varying the speed of recording by tapping tempo instructions almost as you would play the footpedal of a bass drum. So this method of input uses "real-time" in a very generous sense.

Step-Time Recordings

If you are unable to input in real-time, or if you just don't want to (if, for example, you want more time to think between notes) you can put notes in one at a time, either from your electronic keyboard or from the computer keyboard. On the "piano," you press the note you want on the keyboard and with a footpedal or at the computer select the duration of the note. On the computer keyboard, you "spell" the note and indicate duration. Step-time is slow but it allows plenty of careful decision-making and revision in the process.

If your sequencer is connected to a synthesizer, you can listen to any part of your sequence at any time, at any tempo, with any voices your synthesizer provides. This synthesizer might be a card in your computer or an independent "sound module"; most of us use keyboards that are also synthesizers so we input and playback on the same device.

If you are at home with a good word processor, you know that its ease of editing encourages you to revise much more than you did on the typewriter; try it, dump it, move it, enlarge it, stand it on its head. It's all so easy that it makes you consider your options more thoroughly. It's the same with a sequencer. It is so easy to change pitch, tempo, keys, note duration, attack, release, volume, etc. that you can't resist playing with them. And from playfulness springs creativity.

Scanning

The latest input development is a software program that makes it possible for computer scanners (which have previously dealt only with text and graphic images) to "read" printed music. The only such program now available is Musitek's Midiscan. Lay a sheet of music on a page scanner or pass a hand scanner over it; Midiscan will take that information through several automated transformations and produce a MIDI song file which can be imported to your sequencer. This makes the circle of possibilities complete: you can begin at the keyboard and end with a computer-controlled musical performance or sheet music. You can begin with printed music and end with performance or recording. You can get in and out of the process at almost any point. Whatever you have at the start can lead to live or recorded performance.

Do you worry that computers might be unsubtle, mechanical? Just the opposite is true. With a good sequencer, you can modify the length of notes in increments of hundredths, which allows you to escape from the simplistic (intellectual) notion of eighth notes, quarter notes, and such, to the more immediately musical and much more discriminating standard of your ear. Musicality, they tell us, lies in the minute variations from regularity. Heaven, as they say, is in the details. The sequencer/synthesizer is capable of producing nuances as well as the finest virtuoso. Of course your taste must equal the virtuoso's and it will take you a lot more time on the computer.

Notating

Another important piece of music software is the Music Notation program, usually called a notator. A notator allows you to turn your song files into printed music. The top of the line in this field is Finale. It can produce finished pages of music which are acceptable to any music publisher including the most esoteric kinds of notation and symbols. Even the entry-level notators print music that is legible and attractive enough for almost any use.

A notator will print all or part of a file. It will produce full scores or single parts. The size of notes and staves can be varied within a very wide range. Many page-layout and type styles are available in most programs.

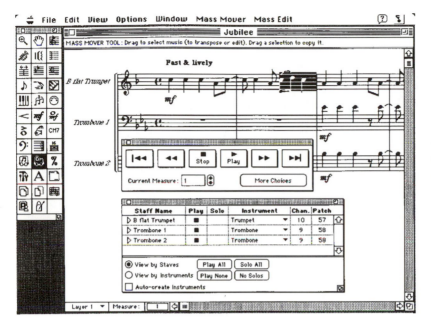

A sample screen from a sequencer/notator program called "Finale."

You can play your music into a notator or step it in just as you would a sequencer. You can copy your sequenced song file to computer disc and mail it across the country to a friend who will print it there. If you don't have that much time, you can export your song file from the sequencer, through a modem, along the phone lines to the modem of your colleague whose notator will print it out instantly. You can carry the score of your favorite musical with you in the breast pocket of your shirt without making a lump and you can print it out whenever you are near a notator and get the urge.

Integrated Sequencer/Notator Programs

If you want to produce tapes or CDs of the finest performance quality, you will need an independent sequencer. If you want to publish your music properly, you will need an independent notator. Most purposes, however, are very well served by programs which integrate the sequencing and notating functions. The software publishers are moving very rapidly in this direction and we will soon have the best of both worlds in these integrated programs. Meanwhile, such integrated programs as Musicator GS for Windows (which I use) meet both needs very nicely.

Love Letters Theme 1

by Roger Gross

Sample of the output of a good notator program quality, *Musicator.*

Synthesizers

To perform your song files, you need a synthesizer. I have used this word in its broader sense to refer to electronic musical instruments with stored voices (also called timbres), which can be played either by a keyboard or by signals from a MIDI sequencer. Some of these machines offer voices that have been constructed from basic sound waves electronically generated. Some offer voices that have been "sampled"; that is, they have been "heard" in the real world by the sampler, analyzed and reconstructed electronically. Some even include the sampling mechanism so that you can capture sounds you hear and turn them into electronic voices. The more "etherial" voices we often associate with electronic music are produced by the synthesizing devices. The most convincing imitations of "real" instruments are found on sampling devices. Much the TV and popular music that sounds "real" to us is actually played on a sampler.

Theatre composing requires me to have one of each. One song file might simultaneously play through both machines. If you choose well, one multi-timbral device should meet your needs. Base your selection on the number and quality of the voices it provides, on the number of channels it can serve, and on the ease of assigning the voices to specific MIDI channels. A full orchestration of a musical might require sixteen different sequencer channels, each with its own set of musical lines. You make these voice assignments in your synthesizer. A good synthesizer should accept external voice cards, making it possible for you to expand your voice library substantially and to keep up with the constantly improving quality of voices.

These are the components of a basic electronic music system. You might want to add some niceties such as an editor/librarian program that keeps things in order for you, makes it easy to reorganize your material, and allows you to easily modify the voices of your synthesizer but it is not really necessary.

So What Can You Do With It?

Plenty. Learning, rehearsal, and performance can all be simplified and enhanced by thoughtful use of this system. In my experience, the thing that excites directors first is the ease of transposition. In the Big Time, they just cast the right actor with the right voice. Most of us face tough compromises: the perfect actress but her range is a third too low. Automatic question: could we transpose it? Automatic answer: do you know how much it costs to transpose? End of hope. With this system, transposition is easy. Have your pianist play the parts into the sequencer one at a time: transpose the whole thing instantaneously by pressing a couple of key; assign the desired voice to each part; tell the notator to print the parts and in a very short time you will be ready to perform without strain or embarrassment. This feature also makes it possible to find the perfect key for each song for each performer. "Can you sing it in this key?" is too crude a question. Try a half-dozen possibilities (in a few minutes) and you'll know which is ideal.

Learning

Every year fewer of our actors can read music. Sad but true. It has become almost standard procedure to provide informal song-learning tapes to each performer. These can be pretty crude and it takes too long to prepare them (usually with a cheap boom box and a built-in microphone). Hard to listen to; hard to hear clearly.

Now we can simply have our pianist play the score into the sequencer. Very quickly, we can produce learning tapes to order. It is a good idea to make two tapes: one of the melody with the accompaniment and one with melody only or with melody and a rhythm beat. If you use a different voice for the melody than for the accompaniment, the tape will be easier to understand.

Another sad story is how few times singers get to work with the orchestra before performance. Too many aural surprises can throw a performer off in a big way. If you spend a little more time at the computer, you can assign voices to the full orchestration as they will be in the live orchestra and provide the performer with a tape that sounds very much like what she'll actually hear in performance. This greatly enhances the performers' security.

Of course the performers should know how to read music. And their pitch should be precise. And they should play the piano. But most of them don't. The computer can help here too; it may offer a way of turning the tide of musical ignorance. There are several outstanding music training programs available. They teach music notation, sight singing; they develop pitch perception; they teach piano technique and music theory. You wouldn't think we would need these things but experience seems to demonstrate that most people learn faster and better from computers. Some of these programs are ingenious and a few are actually fun. They should be used in Musical Theatre classes for those who aren't already prepared.

Rehearsing

The tradition of musical theatre calls for a faithful rehearsal accompanist who, until tech week, provides the only instrumental music the performers hear. The bad news is that these wonderful people are harder to find every year, they cost more, and they have less patience with the endless waiting and repetition. If one or more of these problems makes live rehearsal accompaniment impractical, try your computer music system. Pump the orchestration or the piano part or a small combo into the sequencer. Take your computer in one hand and your synthesizer under the other arm and head for rehearsal. (This is why you should use a notebook or laptop computer. This system works best with a 386-25 or equivalent computer or faster.) The system is cheaper than an accompanist, never calls in sick or gets a paying gig, and isn't bothered by the waiting and the repetition. It plays the number the same way every time unless you want it played differently.

A major advantage is the ease and speed of making changes or starting over or skipping ahead. Oh, the pain I've seen on the faces of dancers and their captains as they struggle to find the beginning of the taped number yet again. The computer will jump instantly to any song location with a couple of keystrokes. Tempo can be varied just as easily. Parts can be added or subtracted at will. The savings in time and stress and the gain in accuracy are amazing.

Rehearsal Scores

Music Theatre International, one of the leading leasors of "Broadway" musical shows, has pioneered a commercial version of the rehearsal system described above. David Pogue, himself a leader in the electronic music field, has so far sequenced eleven of the most popular shows in their catalog:

Annie	*The Apple Tree*
Baby	*The Boyfriend*
Candide	*Closer Than Ever*
Company	*Damn Yankees*
Evita	*Fame: the Musical*
The Fantasticks	*Fiddler on the Roof*
A Funny Thing Happened on the Way to the Forum	*Guys and Dolls*

How to Succeed in Business Without Really Trying	*Into the Woods*
A Little Night Music	*The Music Man*
Once on This Island	*The Pajama Game*
Pirates of Penzance	*Pippin*
Seven Brides for Seven Brothers	*1776*
Singing in the Rain	*Sweeney Todd*
West Side Story	*The World Goes Round (Songs of Kander & Ebb)*

By January 1995, these titles will have been added:

Annie Warbucks	*The Baker's Wife*
The Goodbye Girl	*The Most Happy Fella*
She Loves Me	

If you lease one of these shows from them, you may also lease what they call a Rehearscore: a computer disk with the entire piano score brilliantly performed and recorded as a set of MIDI song files. This disk can be imported into your sequencer and played back by your synthesizer. They have the same flexibility and usefulness of the homemade files I recommended. The lease agreement allows the Rehearscore to be used only for learning and rehearsal. Use in performance is strictly forbidden. Music Theatre International intends to continue producing these Rehearscores at the rate of six to ten per year until their entire catalog has been covered.

It is also possible to buy disks with MIDI-file versions of pop, rock, and show tunes from several commercial sources (which you will find in the classified sections of such specialty magazines as *Electronic Musician*). Lounge singers use a lot of these. You might find them useful for building musical revues. Not surprisingly, they are called "sequences." Just import them into your sequencer and do what you will with them.

Performance

This is a touchier issue for some of us. Of course we want live music in performance, for many reasons. When we can't get an orchestra (or an adequate orchestra) as happens with greater frequency, our alternatives have been to do a one or two piano version (which can work but robs the audience of one of the major thrills of musical theatre) or we, forgive us, use a taped orchestration (which is known as "the really rotten" solution because of inflexibility and fragility, which can cause disasters, and obviously electronic sound quality.)

If you are trapped in such a situation, consider using your computer music system. First, you'll get a much better recording of the orchestration than you would by other means. Then, the sequencer is much less likely to break or malfunction and it is much quicker and easier to lead back from problems when they do occur. Tape's problem of inflexibility, the inability to adapt to changing performance conditions, is pretty much solved by the electronic system: the two "tap tempo" sequencer programs allow you to "conduct" the performance, to control tempo, start, stop, sustain in performance. to approximate the subtlety with which a good orchestra adapts. When sequenced music is played directly through a good theatre sound system, the sound quality is surprisingly immediate and pleasing.

Top-line sequence programs, by the way, can also be used to simultaneously control music and lighting. Touring rock-and-roll extravaganzas have pioneered this use with success that makes most musical theatre seem a bit unimaginative. Sequencer-controlled lighting can produce a visual show with as much control subtlety as music is capable of.

Other Wonders

Some of the things the new music software can do are astonishing. Here are some samples:

Band-in-a-Box-Professional is an automatic accompanist. Type in the chord names for any song, select a style (from the list of 100 styles), and this program will create a combo accompaniment. *The Jammer* will create an appropriate chord pattern and accompaniment for any melody you record. *Sound Globs* improvises music and then allows you to "nudge" it from almost any direction until it pleases you, by which time it has become (in some strange new sense) "your composition." *Vivace* is a new hardware/software combo intended to assist practice: standard repertoire numbers are played while you play long. Amazingly, the band "hears you" and changes tempo to keep in stride with you. If you stop, it stops; if you skip, it skips.

These are just a few of the many new programs which aim to make the musicians life easier and more productive and to open up new creative vistas. But this is just the beginning. Within five years we will see wonders far beyond what we're longing for today. I think anyone seriously interested in musical theatre had better, if only in self-defense, become familiar with these resources, learn how to use them, and consider the potential to enhance the musical theatre experience from start to finish.

And a Warning

When you produce published musicals, you enter the murky world of copyright laws. I have never met two people who interpret the law in the same way. If you ask a leasor, you will hear an interpretation that makes a criminal of you and most of your colleagues in the musical theatre. Many common and seemingly essential practices *may* be illegal. The computer music systems and the practices they enable are so new that it is not possible to say confidently just what is legal and what isn't. The matter is complicated by the unwritten rules which say that some practices which are technically illegal are, in many situations, allowable. For example, you can't legally sing any copyrighted song in public without permission and payment of royalty. But we do and if we don't do it for profit, nothing comes of it . . . usually.

I am not qualified to interpret the law for you, to tell you what you may reasonably and safely do. As you always have, you must use your own best judgement with full awareness that the copyright law exists. When in serious doubt, it is best to consult an attorney.

Law always lags behind the times. It always fails to protect some who need help and, in its clumsiness and over-generalization, gets in the way of reasonable people to the advantage of no one. Those of us who care about musical theatre and who see these great new opportunities on the horizon should band together to encourage reasonable interpretation and modification of the law.

Resources: Books

Greg R. Starr's *What's a Sequencer?* and Jon F. Eiche's *What's MIDI?* are very breezily written, entry-level books on the fundamentals; short, cute, useful. Both were published in 1990 so they are just slightly behind the market. More comprehensive treatments are provided by Joseph Rothstein in *MIDI: a Comprehensive Introduction* (1992) and by Jeff Rona in *MIDI: The Ins, Outs, and Thrus* (1992).

When you get into computer/music work, the first major decision you must make is whether to go with Macintosh or PC (IBM Compatibles). There are other options but these are the best. Some programs exist in versions for either format but many written for one or the other. Here are a few very good books that are "dedicated" to one format: *The Musical PC* edited by Geary Yelton (1992), seems to me to be the best available for any system. It describes and evaluates the major programs and equipment, advises on buying and using a system. Yelton also wrote *Music and the Macintosh* (1989) and Christopher Yavelow provided *Macworld Music and Sound Bible* (1992).

The Mix Bookshelf (6400 Hollis St., Suite #12, Emeryville, CA 94608) provides a very efficient buying service for music books of all types, including extensive coverage of computer/music systems. They will send a free catalog.

Music software (at discount prices) and extremely useful, free advice is available from Soundware. Call 800-333-4554 for a free catalog.

The best of the popular sequencing programs are Cakewalk Pro, Sequencer Plus, Master Tracks Pro and Cadenza (all for IBM/Compatibles) and Performer, Vision, and Master Tracks 5 (for Macintosh). The best of the integrated sequencer/notators for IBM Compatibles are Finale, Encore, Musicator, Music Prose (simpler version of Finale) and Music Printer Plus. Three of these (Finale, Encore, Music Prose) make versions for Macintosh. There are several useful entry-level integrated programs (e.g., Quickscore Deluxe and SongWright) which sell for much less.

The computer/music field is developing so rapidly that books are always a bit behind. The best way to keep up with new opportunities is through music magazines such as *Electronic Musician* and *Keyboard* or such computer publications as *PC Magazine, PC World*, or *Macworld*.

Glossary

Action—The energy released in working a problem; the interplay between actors. Viola Spolin, *Improvisation for the Theatre* (Northwestern University Press, 1983).

Apron—The part of the stage in front of the act curtain.

Beat—A component of action or intention within a scene; can be any length.

Black light—A special light that, when projected onto a dark background, picks up fluorescent paint or white, and causes it to seem to glow.

Blocking—where actors move on given lines, words, or actions.

Book—(Libretto) Dialogue or part of a musical that is spoken, not sung.

Callback—After the director has seen, heard and read all actor/singers, some are brought back for final tryouts.

Casting against type—Using an actor or actress not just for how they look but how well they act/sing.

Character's emotional center (see also Spine)—Traits that form the character's person.

Characterization—The endowment of a role with particular traits and behavioral patterns (which the actor imagines) belonging specifically to that character and creating a past for the character.

Concentration—The state of being connected to, united with.

Concept—Choices made by actors and directors using change to further the action (i.e., laughter, tears to help unify the vision of piece).

Costume parade—when the director looks at all costumes together usually before a dress rehearsal.

Dress rehearsal—Final rehearsal with sets, costumes, makeup, lights, sound, etc.

Drop—A curtain that can be lowered in place with a set painted on it; usually used so you can change the furniture behind it and quickly go on to the next scene.

Dry tech—Rehearsal with no actors, just crew and designers, stage manager and director.

Focus—Directing and concentrating attention on a specific person, object, or event within the stage reality; to frame a person, object, or event on stage. From Viola Spolin, *Improvisation for the Theatre* (Northwestern University Press, 1983).

Flat—A light wooden or metal frame covered by canvas and used for scenery.

Hell Week—Last week before opening.

Improvisation or to improvise—Setting out to solve a problem with no pre-conception as to how you will do it; permitting everything in the environment (animate or inanimate) to work for you in solving the problem; not the scene, but the way to the scene; bringing forth details and relationships as an organic whole (based on Spolin workshop at American Theatre Association).

Motivation—That which induces; gives incentives; the state or acts of being.

Objective—What you are trying to accomplish, attain; the purpose.

Off book—When actors have their lines memorized and no longer carry a script.

Pace—The energy and speed with which a play or scene moves forward to the finale.

Physicalization—Showing rather than telling; the physical expression of giving life.

Picking up cues—To increase the playing pace by shortening the interval between cues.

Recitative—Rhythmically free vocal style of dramatic speaking, first used in the early 17th Century, imitating the natural speech rhythms; used for dialogue and narrative passages.

Rhythm (not musical rhythm)—The acceleration or diminution of inner intensity; the external manifestation is pace.

Scrim—A drop made of fabric that becomes transparent when lit from behind but is opaque when lit from the front.

Set dressing—The furniture, rugs, and wall decorations that make the set look three-dimensional.

Spine—Backbone; a trait; a quality that constitutes a principal strength or need that drives the character throughout the play.

Subtext—A term common to the Stanislavski system. Refers to the meaning underlying dialogue and stage directions. Subtext may include invented autobiographical material about a character provided that is clearly related to the text and not merely arbitrary. Dr. Jerry Crawford *Acting in Person and in Style* (Wm. C. Brown, 1980).

Timing—The art of delivering words or performing movement at the effective instant. Dr. Jerry Crawford *Acting in Person and in Style* (Wm. C. Brown, 1980).

Vakhtangov, Yevgeny—Stanislavski's trusted associate and a major director/teacher in his own right.

Warning cue—What the SM puts in his/her book so (s)he will know when to communicate directions to the crew and cast. (Warning cues are usually marked one page prior to actual cue.)

Recommended Reading/
Other Resources

Benedetti, Robert. *The Actors Work*. Prentice Hall, 1990.

Brook, Peter. *Empty Space*. Macmillan, 1978

Brockett, Oscar. *History of the Theatre*. Allyn & Bacon, 1990

Buckman, Herman. *Stage Makeup*. New York: Back Stage Books, 1988.

Chekhov, Michael. *On the Technique of Acting*. Harper Collins, 1985.

Clurman, Harold. *On Directing*. Macmillan, 1974.

Cole, Tobe. *Actors on Acting*. Crown, 1970.

Craig, David. *On Stage Singing*. Applause Books, 1990

Craig, David. *On Performing, A Handbook for Actors, Dancers, Singers on Stage*. McGraw Hill, 1989.

Crawford, Jerry. *Acting in Person and in Style*. William C. Brown, 1980.

Dean, Alexander and Lawrence Cara. *Fundamentals of Play Directing*. Holt Rinehart & Winston, 1989.

Dychtwald, Ken and Joe Flower, *Age Wave—The Challenge of Aging America*. Jeffery Tarcher, Inc, 1990.

Engel, Lehman. *Getting the Show On*. Schumer Books, 1983.

Gorchakov, N. *Stanislavski Directs Opera*. Greenwood, 1954.

Grote, David. *Staging a Musical*. Simon & Schuster, 1986.

Hagen, Uta. *A Challenge for the Actor*. Macmillan, 1991.

Housman, John. *Unfinished Business*. Applause Books, 1989.

Lewis, Robert. *Method or Madness*. Samuel French, 1958.

Machlen, Evangeline. *Dialects for the Stage*. (Available with audiocassette.) Theater Arts Books, 1975.

McGaw, Charles and Larry Clark. *Acting Is Believing*. Holt Rinehart & Winston, 1986.

Olsen, Mark. *The Golden Buddha Changing Masks*. Gateway Publishing, 1984.

Richards, Stanley. *Great Musicals of the American Theatre, Vol. 2*. Chilton Books, 1973.

Sabatine, Jean. *Actors Image*. Backstage Books, 1994.

Seyler, Athene. *The Craft of Comedy*. Theatre Arts, 1957.

Spolin, Viola. *Improvisations for the Theatre*. Northwestern University Press, 1983.

Spolin, Viola. *Theatre Games for Rehearsal*. Northwestern University Press, 1985.

Stanislavski, Constantin. *An Actor Prepares*. New York: A Theater Arts Book, Routeledge, 1989.

Stanislavski, Constantin. *Building A Character*. New York: A Theater Arts Book, Routledge, 1989.

Stanislavski. *An Actor's Handbook*. Elizabeth Reynolds Hapgood, editor and translator. New York: Theatre Arts, 1963.

Sullivan, Jan. *The Phenomenon of Belt/Pop Voice*. Brigham Young University, Provo, Utah.

Yakim, Moni. *Creating a Character*. Backstage Books, 1990.

Young, David. *Audience Development*. Theatre for the Community Series, 1981, Penn State University.

Suggested Reading for the Staff

Theatre Crafts Magazine, 135 Fifth Avenue, NY, NY 10010

Stage Directions, P.O. Box 1966, West Sacramento CA 95691

About the Author

David Young was for over fifteen years the Producing Director of the American College Theater Festival (ACTF) at the John F. Kennedy Center for the Performing Arts, Washington, D.C. ACTF is a national educational theatre program involving more than 450 colleges and universities in its network and having an audience numbering more than one million annually.

Prior to coming to Washington David Young was artistic director of the Mark Twain Masquers, a community theatre in Hartford, Connecticut, and was for many years a professional actor, appearing on NBC-TV's "Medallion Theatre" with Richard Kiley, off Broadway with Anne Meara, and on tour with Colleen Dewhurst.

He has taught classes in directing, acting, and musical theatre in the U.S., Brazil, the People's Republic of China, Sengal, and Greece and at the University of Hartford and the Hartford Conservatory. He is a guest lecturer for the Smithsonian Institution.

Beginning his career with Erwin Piscator, the noted German director, at the Dramatic Workshop at the New School for Social Research in New York, Dr. Young holds a Ph.D. from Columbia Pacific University. He is a member of Actors Equity Association, the Society of Stage Directors and Choreographers, and the Association for Theatre in Higher Education. He is also a past president of the American Community Theatre Association (now AACT); a recipient of the American Association of Community Theater National Patrons Award; and has been elected to College of Fellows of the American Theatre.

Off Broadway David Young directed Trish Van Devere in her New York debut and co-produced and acted in a pre-Broadway tryout of a play *Angel on the Loose,* starring Arthur Treacher. Dr. Young has directed almost one hundred productions, including many musicals, his favorites being *Most Happy Fella, Guys and Dolls, Company, Grease, Fanny,* and *The Boyfriend.* His latest non-musical directing assignments have been *Amadeus, Foxfire, Monday after the Miracle,* and *Steel Magnolias.* He has also directed over thirty original plays.

Additionally, he has been a lecturer at the American Association of State Colleges and Universities and a national judge for the National Society of Arts and Letters. He was a founding member of the Helen Hayes Awards in Washington, D.C., served as artistic adviser (theatre) for the Presidential Scholars in the Arts, and is listed in *Who's Who in American Theatre.*

As this book goes to press, Dr. Young is the graduate research professor in the Theatre Department at the University of Florida (UF), Gainesville, Florida.

Index

Note: for entries with roman numerals I, II, III, IV, and V, refer to the appropriate index.

A
accents 64
 pitch 9
 realism 79
acting 49–60, I, II, III
 Actor's Equity 114
 aging actors 65–66
aging 6, 65, 79
Ajax 113
A Little Night Music 144
Anything Goes 11, 42
Aspects of Love 2, 11
A Streetcar Named Desire 51
Atkinson, Brooks xvi
audience 2, 8, 17, 19, 27, 34, 37, 43, 54, 59, 69, 76, 82, 86, 88, 91, I, III, IV
 building 1, 65, 66, 154
auditions 25–30, 97, 99, 105

B
Balanchine, George 23

Barr, Tony 55
beats 8, 22, 23, 50, 102
Berhman, S. N. xviii
Berlin, Irving 10, 46
blending 32, 75, 133
blocking 3, 18, 19, 36–38, 41, 54, 59, 61, 66, 67, 73, 81, I, IV
 shorthand 53
Boyer, Charles 29
Branden, Nathaniel 55
Broadway 2, 91, 116, 143

C
Cabaret 2, 126, 127, 132
Carnival 13, 42
Caron, Leslie 29
Carousel xviii, 9
Carra, Lawrence 38
casting 25–30
 callbacks 28–29
 children I
 disabled II

final callbacks 30
notice 25, 28
resumes 26
characterization xviii, 56–58, 59, 63,
77, 85, 117, 149
exercises 51, 58
listening 55
Chekhov, Michael 102, 153
checklist 7
Chess 42
Chicago 124
children I
choreography IV
choreographer 21
sculpting 21
singing 115, 130
untrained dancers VI
City of Angels 2, 11
Clark, Larry 7, 154
climax 53, 70, 89, 130
Cohen, Robert 9
collaboration 20, 21, 75
comedy 8, 62–63, 116, 119, 125,
127, 128, 154
timing 63
Company 11, 143, 156
computer technology V
concentration 75, 77–79, 133, 149
exercise 79
costumes 12–14, 82
design 116, 122, 123, 125
parade 150
planning 14
research 125
Craig, David 9, 153
Crawford, Jerry 151, 153
Crawford, Joan 7
Crazy for You 11
crew 12, 18, 34, 66, 150
curtain call 81, 88

D
dance 1, 2, 21, 23, 26, 32, 75, 123,
125–127, 128
Dean, Alexander 38, 153
Death of a Salesman 77
Desert Song 2, 5
Dewhurst, Colleen 26, 156
dialogue 2, 7, 50, 85, 102, 106, 117,
128, 151
diary 3–4
directing xvi, IV, 153
activity 18, 49, I, IV
definition 49
director xvi, 3–4, 21, 23, 26, 28, 33,
37, 58–59, 76, 79, 80, 82, 91, I, II,
III, IV
assistant 26, 33, 37, 60, 66
musical 6, 7, 20, 26, 28, 66
relationship with actor 9, 27, 54, I
director's book 3, 37, 41
disabled actors II
Doors 102, 108

E
effects, theatrical 6
emotion 50, 56, 72, 87
ensembles 121
evaluation 90–91
sample 91
Evans, Barbara xiv
Evita 11, 143

F
Fanny xv, 1, 3, 8, 9, 12, 25, 35, 53,
57, 60, 62, 63, 64, 72, 74, 80, 84
as song title 3, 17, 73
plot outline of 4–6
staging 39–42
farce 62–63, 123
feedback 28, 49, 103

Fiddler on the Roof 2, 127, 143
fights, stage 63–64
   Society of American Fight
   Directors 63
flexibility 27, 53
focus 37, 150
Follies 122
Fontanne, Lynn 77
Freedman, Gerald 49
Funny Girl 126
*Funny Thing Happened on the Way to
   the Forum* VI

G
George M 122
Gershwin, George 10, 46, 47, 48
Gilbert and Sullivan 118
Grand Hotel 2, 42
Grease 5, 132, 156
guide 1–3

H
Hagen, Uta 52, 153
Hammerstein, Oscar 10
Harlem Renaissance 43
Hello Dolly 127
Henderson, Florence xv
Hoffman, Dustin 77–78, 106

I
improvisation 150
   character building 59–60
   children I
intensity 18, 69, 71, 89, 96
intermision 41, 82, 87

K
Kennedy Center 49, 77, 78, 90, 113,
   155
Kline, Kevin 41

L
language, body 51, 114
licensing agencies 1, 2
Lighthouse, the 114
lighting 86, 145
   design 17, 44, 199
   tech rehearsal 18
Little Man Tate 108
Little Match Girl, the 97, 98, 99
listening 55
   exercise 55–56
Loesser, Frank 10
Logan, Joshua xiii
lyrics 2, 7, 45, 50, 52, 115
   spoken 11

M
makeup 17, 113, 127, 153
   artist 17
   design 17
Mame 2
Man of La Mancha 124
Martin, Mary xv
Meisner, Sanford 51
Merry Widow, the 5
microphone 66s
Miller, James 21, 22, 121, 122, 126,
   129
minorities 43
Miss Saigon 2, 42
Mother Hicks I
motivation 6, 7, 75, 104, 105, 125,
   130, 150
movement III, IV
music 1, 2, 9, 10, 11, 18, 22, 23, 34,
   43, 61, 91, III, IV, V
   action 37, 41, 51, 52
   director 6, 20, 30, 33, 86, 74
   research 126, 127
musical categories 1, 2

musical revue 43
Music Man xvi, 42, 118, 144
My Fair Lady 122, 123, 127, 128

N
National Information Center on
 Deafness 114
National Theatre of the Deaf 109,
 110
need 50, 75, 151
notes (sample) 34, 68

O
objective 50, 150
Odets, Clifford 10
Oklahoma 2
opening night 60, 75, 88, 80 , 114
orchestra 88, 142, 144, 145
 rehearsal 20, 66–67
Osterhaus, Carveth 22, 23

P
pacing 70, 71–80
Pajama Game 116, 117, 118, 144
Panisse, sample autobiography 34
Patinkin, Mandy 41
pauses 7, 70, 71, 72, 79, 82
performing I
Phantom of the Opera 2, 11
photographs 9, 26, 80
pianist 20, 141, 142
Pinza, Ezio xv
Pirandello, Luigi 10
pitch 64, 142
playwriting, children I
plot 4, 6, 74, 75, 115, 119, 122, 129
Porter, Cole 9, 10
preview 88
production book 18, 19
production meeting 12, 18
property master 18

props 18, 19, 73, 116, 117
publicity 80

R
Racing with the Clock 118
rehearsal 17, 18, 49, 54, 58, 60, 74,
 82, I, II, IV, V
 children I
 demonstrating 101
 dress 87, 89
 first 31–48
 midway 51–70
 modeling 101
 organizing 1, 2, 7, 12, 52, 79
 pianist 20
 relaxers 87
 run through 68
 scheduling 29, 30, 31, 53
 special 73, 89
 technical 69
relating 33, 54
relaxation 61, 67, 89
reviews 90, 91
rhythm 6, 22, 128, 142, 150
Robber Bridegroom, The 123
Rodgers, Richard 8, 9, 10
Rome, Harold xiii

S
Sabatine, Jean 87, 154
sample notes 68
script 18, 19, 50, 117, I, III, IV
 analysis 7, 8, 76
 concept 37
 memorization 54, 59
 for children I
sculpting 21
Seago, Howie 113
Sellars, Peter 64, 113
senior citizens 65, 123
senses 50, 55

sets 15, 82
  designer 116
Seyler, Athene 62, 63, 154
singers 9, 10, 11, 20, 51, 52, 64, 66,
    71, 73, 79, 83, I, IV, V
Slezak, Walter xv
Sondheim, Stephen 2, 9
songs, organization of 2, 8, 85, III,
    IV
sound 17, 81, V
  cues 19
  designer 17, 86
  microphones 66
  special effects V
Sound of Music xv, 42, 94
South Pacific 11
spine xvii, 57, 68, 151
Spolin, Viola 52, 154
stage manager 7, 18, 19, 37, 81, 82,
    113
staging 6, 21, 22, 37, 39–44, 48,
    63–64, 88, III, IV
Stand by Me 108
Stanislavski, Konstantin 154
  characterization 52, 57
  children I
  motivation 75
  opera 153
  subtext 7, 151
  system xvii, 7, 94
Step on a Crack 100, 108, I
Stop the World, I Want to Get Off 128
Strasberg, Lee 7, 50
streamlining 71–80
style 3, 9–11

  definition 9
subplot 5
subtext 7, 50, 75, 83, 151

T
teens I
tempo 115, 117, 137, 143, 145
theatre, musical xvi
timing 63, 73, 82, 151
To Kill a Mockingbird 94
transposing music 135, V
Tulane Summer Lyric Theatre 121, IV
Tune, Tommy 4

V
Vakhtangov, Yevgeny 52, 151
Verry Good Eddie 123, 124, 132
Very Special Arts 114
videotape 79
Vunovich, Nancy 42, 115

W
warm-up 33
West Side Story xvii, 123, 144
wigs 12
Willard, Charlie 76
Williams, Tennessee 51
Willis, Ronald 76
Witness 108
Wrinkle in Time 101

Y
Yakim, Moni 75, 154